INTRODUCTION

I love debauched food. You know the sort: seared, crunchy goodness you need to chomp on the entire day. But making these foods can be time-consuming and messy, and you don't want to eat them regularly because of their high fat content. I'm a bustling mother of three and a business person, so my days are full from the second my feet hit the floor every morning. I don't have the opportunity to go the entire day in the kitchen cooking and cleaning. But sometimes I just have to surrender to my cravings, and that's where the air fryer comes in.

When I initially began utilizing the air fryer, it was scaring, and I did not know what I was doing. I struggled accepting anybody could make quality food in a ledge apparatus. But the more I worked with it, the more I realized how versatile it was. Air browning the food sources my family needed took less time than customary singing, and the outcome was better. The air fryer immediately became one of my most-utilized apparatuses, and I even got one for my camper and one more for my child's apartment.

The more I utilize the air fryer, the more I love it. Little kitchen machines should make suppers simple and moderately speedy to get ready. Indeed, saving time was my principle center while making the plans for this book. They are planned to make you consider some fresh possibilities with regards to air broiling, and they might even motivate you to make your own air-singed treats.

I normally incline toward plans that call for fixings I as of now have available, and you likely do, as well. I shared a great deal of those plans in my first air fryer book

The air fryer is ideal for preparing little suppers, and it dispenses with the requirement for a broiler. It's additionally an incredible device for making family dinners when you are tight on schedule. Or on the other hand perhaps you very love firm, crunchy food as I do. Regardless you use your air fryer for, this book has you covered.

Keep an eye out for the "Can You Fry It?" notes all through this book. They educate you to food sources you may never envision air browning, as pancakes
and lobster tails. Is it true or not that you are prepared to begin? We should get frying!

CHAPTER 1
FEED YOUR AIR

FRYER OBSESSION

Whether the air fryer is a new captivation or you're a prepared fry-head, this book is for you. It incorporates 129 delectable plans, in addition to valuable tips and innovative motivation. Assuming you're a relative novice, this book gives you a lot of fast and simple plans to kick you off. More experienced cooks will observe new takes on the works of art you've been making for quite a long time. I trust these fun and inventive plans will before long be among your top choices. My objective is so that you might be able to see the practically perpetual capability of the air fryer and for you to cherish cooking with it as much as I do.

5 Reasons I'm Obsessed with My Air Fryer

1. Air singing is preferred for you over ordinary searing. Its an obvious fact that broiled food sources are higher in fat. There are an incredible 9 calories in each gram of fat, which makes it truly difficult to keep calories low while partaking in your beloved pan fried food sources. The air fryer is mystical on the grounds that definitely decreasing the oil additionally slices your caloric intake.
2. Air searing keeps cleanup simple. Many air fryer plans require just a blending bowl or two preceding you add the food to the bin, so you dispense with the requirement for huge baking sheets, enormous stockpots, and a ton of dishes. Reward: If you use material liners in your air fryer, it's significantly simpler to clean the basket.
3. Air fricasseeing saves energy. I love that I can make all my most loved singed, prepared, and cooked food varieties without turning on the stove. This is particularly great throughout the late spring months, when I can keep the entire house cooler without undermining my menu.
4. Air fryers are extraordinary for inexpensively, dinners. At the point when my child set off for college, I tried to outfit him with a little air fryer and my first air fryer cookbook, *The Essential Air Fryer Cookbook for Two*.

He had the option to make nutritious dinners in spite of having almost no counter space, and he set aside cash by eating out less frequently.
5. The air fryer isn't only for broiling. It works like a small scale convection broiler, so you can utilize it to plan nearly anything you would typically make in a customary stove, from canapés like seared mozzarella sticks, to principle dishes like honey-prepared ham, to pastries like chocolate magma cakes. Air singing assists you with thinking outside the customary box while you're making speedy, simple, better recipes.

What's Your Fry Style?

There are a few kinds of air fryers available, which is a major change over late years. There is something for everybody. On the off chance that you're hoping to purchase a new

one, here's a breakdown of what's accessible as of this composition. Search for air fryers that have an advanced showcase to help ensure your temperature and clock settings are exact. Regardless kind of air fryer you have, the plans in this book will be not difficult to make and will taste delicious.

BASKET FRYER

My initial two air fryers were bin style. This type includes a removable container in a cabinet that you embed into the machine prior to cooking. The idea is like a customary profound fryer, however rather than bringing down the bin into a tank of oil, you pop it into the fryer and hot air courses around the food. This model is exceptionally well known, most likely in light of the fact that it arrives in an assortment of sizes, obliging each circumstance from a couple of individuals to a huge family. My child utilizes a bin fryer to make his more modest segments, and we utilize one while setting up camp on the grounds that even the models with a huge limit are still compact.

PADDLE FRYER

The oar or self-mixing air fryer takes the container style to another level. It has a comparative look and a drop-in bushel, yet in addition incorporates an oar that pivots and blends the food as it's cooking, so the fryer requires less consideration and creates all the more uniformly prepared food. The oar fryer is typically more costly than the crate fryer.

OVEN-STYLE FRYER

The stove style fryer is my new fixation. I got one since I love that it has a window toward the front so I can see the food while it's cooking. This model has additional features, such as double wire racks for maximizing space, rotating wire drums for tossing things like French fries while they are cooking, and optional accessories for cooking dishes like a rotisserie-style chicken. The broiler style fryer costs about equivalent to the bin fryer.

Air Frying 101

Whether you are new to air fricasseeing or a prepared master, it's smart to go over certain essentials to ensure your plans divert out amazing from the start.

SETUP

No matter what sort of air fryer you have, the initial thing to do is perused the manual and get to know its buttons and features.

When you're cooking, place the machine on a level, level surface away from combustible things like kitchen towels or plastic items that could soften. Most pieces of the machine stay cool during the cooking system, yet the hotness produced inside the machine while cooking gets pushed out through the ventilation parts. Ensure the vents have sufficient room. I like to put my air fryer on a kitchen island or landmass, yet pulling it away from the divider on the kitchen counter works extraordinary, too.

HOW TO USE IT

Most air fryers have a handle or fastens to set the temperature and time. Many likewise have presets for baking or searing. I seldom utilize these presets, as the manual settings for time and temperature yield a similar outcome. A few plans require preheating, so actually take a look at your manual. Preheating by and large makes the food crispier and crunchier than if you begin with a cold fryer.

CLEANING

Before getting everything rolling, utilize a lathery wipe and boiling water to wash all the fryer parts that will interact with your food, including the bushel, the oar, and the wire racks. Allow the fryer to air dry or wipe it with a delicate kitchen towel to ensure everything is totally dry before cooking.

GEEK OUT ON AIR FRYER SCIENCE

The technology behind air frying has been around for a while. Much like convection ovens, air fryers use a high-powered fan to circulate hot air within the cooking area. The fan helps evenly distribute the heat around the food, which results in more uniformly cooked food and reduced cooking times. This process also eliminates cold pockets that can result when cooking in an oven. The quick air circulation distributes fine oil droplets in the air, creating the great crunchy texture we fried-food-lovers crave.

Some air fryers have the ability to go from cool to more than 300 degrees Fahrenheit in a matter of 3 minutes, which is much faster than a conventional oven and eliminates the need for preheating in some recipes. Meal prep is also faster when you don't have to wait for the oven to preheat. Food is suspended in the basket or on the wire racks in an air fryer, so it's easy for the heat to completely surround the food, whereas the bottom of food can be undercooked in the oven.

Tools of the Expert Air Fryer

A modest bunch of apparatuses and frill make air singing more straightforward and can assist with extending your machine's capacities. Here are my top picks, a significant number of which are accessible at retailers across the country and online in helpful, reasonable bundles.

Baking dish: Some plans in this book require little baking skillet that are intended for the air fryer. Baking skillet are much of the time remembered for packs with numerous different things in this list.

Instant-read thermometer: This device has a treated steel test you embed into meat, poultry, fish, and heated products to decide if the food is completely cooked and protected to eat. You can get one for around $10.

Oil sir: Aerosol cooking splash leaves a film on the air fryer that doesn't fall off, so I like to utilize olive oil or other cooking oils, showered by a siphon spritzer or a spurt bottle intended for oil. You will utilize your oil mister much of the time, so get one that functions admirably. These are accessible for under $20.

Parchment liners: I propose covering the air fryer container or rack with a material liner each time you cook with it. This liner lessens cleanup time, holds sauce and more modest food varieties back from falling through the crate openings, and keeps stickier food varieties from baking onto the bin and plate. You can purchase precut liners or cut a customary roll of material paper to fit.

Ramekins: I keep four shallow ramekins and four slightly deeper ramekins on hand. The shallow ones are extraordinary for things like Chocolate Lava Cakes or for making plans like individual omelet cups. I use the deeper ones for recipes like <u>Chocolate Mug Cakes</u> because they take up less space than mugs with handles.

Silicone cupcake liners: Traditional cupcake skillet don't fit in an air fryer, however silicone cupcake liners turn out incredible for making food varieties like cupcakes, egg cups, and muffins.

Tongs: This apparatus makes it a lot more straightforward to deal with hot food sources in restricted spaces like the fry bin. Use utensils to put food in the air fryer, flip food, and eliminate hot food from the appliance.

KNOW YOUR OILS

Air frying creates the same great flavors and textures as deep-frying, but the food is much healthier. This cooking method eliminates most of the oils in recipes, but it's important to use a little spritz of oil in order to get a crispy, crunchy texture. An oil mister or a squirt bottle made for oil is the best tool for the job. Spraying with oil gives food a light, even coating without any excess, so you use a lot less than you would with a deep fryer.

This light oil layer is especially important for recipes that are breaded or coated with bread crumbs or panko, when you want a result as close to deep-fried as possible. I like to keep one bottle filled with avocado, sesame, peanut, or extra-light olive oil for savory dishes and another bottle filled with grape-seed, vegetable, or canola oil for sweeter recipes.

Troubleshooting

Like any machine, the air fryer takes a little becoming acclimated to. Here are probably the most well-known issues you may experience, in addition to guidance to assist you with investigating your concerns as simple as (air-seared) pie.

My new air fryer produces a plastic smell.

Some air fryers radiate a hot plastic smell when you initially begin utilizing them, however this scent should blur after rehashed use. Here is a straightforward stunt to help: Combine 1 tablespoon white vinegar and 1 tablespoon lemon juice in a little hotness safe bowl, like a ramekin. Place the bowl in the air fryer, set the temperature to 370°F, and cook for 2 minutes. This ought to diminish the plastic smell so you can partake in the brilliant aroma of fresh food instead.

My food is dry, soaked, or not crisp.

You are presumably not utilizing sufficient oil. That large number of small oil particles coursing inside the air fryer make the food fresh however not dry, so assuming you need that singed surface, don't skirt the showering step.

My food is half-cooked or overcooked.

Undercooked food is normally the consequence of congestion the bin or plate. Take a stab at working in little bunches and watch out for the food during the most recent couple of minutes. Also, not all air fryers cook the same way. Varieties in size and wattage can influence what amount of time it requires for the machine to cook food varieties. At the point when I'm utilizing another machine, I like to test a modest bunch of plans to measure whether it will in general take a cycle longer or appears to cook quicker than the time determined in the recipe.

My air fryer smells.

The most ideal way to forestall waiting food smells is to clean the air fryer appropriately after each utilization. Eliminate the fryer container and some other extras and wash, flush completely, and dry prior to beginning the following recipe.

White smoke is coming from my air fryer.

White smoke is frequently the consequence of an excess of oil or additional food that has gathered at the lower part of the machine. Between each bunch, make certain to wipe and crash any overabundance food or oil that has fallen under the bushel or on the trickle tray.

Black smoke is coming from my air fryer.

Black smoke shows an issue with the machine. Switch behind closed doors fryer and don't utilize it until an apparatus specialist has fixed it.

About the Recipes

I like cooking to be fun, fascinating, and agreeable, and I needed to remember an unexpected surprise for everybody for this book. You'll observe exemplary plans that have been streamlined for air browning, just as a portion of my top picks that take air searing to an unheard of level. I've added the accompanying marks and tips to the plans for speedy reference.

LABELS

Family Favorite: These plans, which serve no less than 4 individuals and have kid-accommodating fixings, range from works of art made simple to excessively fun treats.

Gluten-Free: Fried food doesn't need to incorporate gluten. I've included plans for the people who are gluten-free.

Super-Fast: When I say super-quick, I mean the entire prep and cooking process takes an aggregate of 15 minutes or less. Presently that is some fast cooking.

Vegetarian: So many individuals need or need to adhere to vegan choices, so I've made a few plans for you, too.

TIPS

Look for these tips all through the book. They will assist you with tracking down different plans to finish your dinner, ways of adjusting plans for more assortment, and thoughts for being more effective during the cooking process.

Change It Up: Quick thoughts for trading out fixings to switch around the flavors and give the formula an alternate spin.

Faster Frying: My best ways to smooth out the interaction to make the formula much quicker and rearrange the meal.

Fry Fact: Fun cooking tips, formula hacks (like how to check for doneness), and valuable wellbeing information.

Pair It With: A speedy reference to different plans in the book that pair well with this one.

CAN YOU FRY IT?

You can make so many things in an air fryer, and you probably haven't even thought of most of them yet. You might wonder if you can cook a certain food in the air fryer, so keep an eye out for quick and easy "Can You Fry It?" mini recipes for unexpected dishes. Air-fried lobster tails, anyone?

Get Cooking and Get Creative

Small kitchen apparatuses are here to make our lives simpler and improve on our time in the kitchen. I made each formula in this book determined to set aside you time and cash and making supper time charming. The fixing records are short, and the prep steps are kept to a minimum.

This book isn't just an asset for supper time necessities yet additionally a wellspring of motivation for cooking the food sources that fulfill you. The air fryer is so flexible. You can adjust every one of the plans to serve less individuals or

twofold them for a greater group. You don't need to adhere to chicken strips, by the same token. This book shows you that it is so natural to make morning meals, sides, principle dishes, better choices, and absurd treats you would never envision emerging from this impressive apparatus. I want to believe that you get as fixated on air broiling as I am.

CHAPTER 2
BREAKFAST

Churro Donut Holes Jelly
Donuts French
Toast Sticks Homemade
Toaster Pastries Gluten-
Free Granola Cereal
Gluten-Free Cinnamon-Raisin Granola Bars
Cinnamon-Raisin Bagels
Banana-Nut Muffins
Cheesy Scrambled Eggs
Hard-Boiled Eggs Puffed
Egg Tarts Easy Hash
Browns Breakfast Hash
Ham and Cheese Crescents
"All the Favorites" Quiche

PUFFED EGG TARTS

CHURRO DONUT HOLES

SUPER-FAST
VEGETARIAN

Serves 4/Prep Time: 5 minutes/Fry Time: 5 minutes

The beginning of churros isn't exactly clear, yet their ubiquity all over the planet, especially in Spain and Portugal, is. In the United States, the singed batter sticks moved in cinnamon-sugar have turned into a staple at fairs and amusement parks. This formula adjusts them into doughnut holes.

Oil, for spraying
1 (12-ounce) can refrigerated buttermilk biscuits
¼ cup sugar
1 tablespoon ground cinnamon

1. Preheat the air fryer to 350°F. Line the air fryer container with material and splash gently with oil.
2. Separate the batter and cut every bread roll into 4 pieces. Daintily roll each piece between your hands to shape them into balls.
3. Place the balls in the pre-arranged bushel and shower delicately with oil. You many need to work in clumps, contingent upon the size of your air fryer.
4. Cook for 4 to 5 minutes, or until carmelized and cooked through.
5. In a little paper pack or a zip-top plastic sack, join the sugar and cinnamon and shake until mixed.
6. Spray the doughnut openings delicately with oil and quickly move to the pack with the cinnamon-sugar combination. Close the pack and shake well to cover the doughnut openings with the mixture.
7. Serve right away. Try not to store the doughnut openings clinched or they will become soggy.

Change It Up: To make a doughnut glaze plunging sauce, blend ¼ cup confectioners' sugar with a sprinkle of milk and race to join. You can likewise disperse ¼ cup jam with a sprinkle of water and hotness it in the microwave for 15 seconds to make a fruity plunging sauce.

Per serving: Calories: 293; Total fat: 8g; Saturated fat: 3g; Cholesterol: 0mg; Sodium: 745mg; Carbohydrates: 51g; Fiber: 3g; Protein: 6g

JELLY DONUTS

SUPER-FAST
VEGETARIAN

Makes 8 doughnuts/Prep Time: 10 minutes/Fry Time: 5 minutes

Jelly doughnuts are here and there alluded to as Bismarck doughnuts in the Midwest. Regardless you call it, the singed round batter loaded up with natural product jam and finished off with sugar or sprinkled with icing is a heavenly method for beginning your day.

Oil, for spraying
1 (16-ounce) can refrigerated huge biscuits
½ cup sugar
8 tablespoons jam of choice
5 tablespoons unsalted margarine, melted

1. Preheat the air fryer to 360°F. Line the air fryer bushel with material and splash softly with oil.
2. Separate the batter into 8 pieces.
3. Place the mixture in the arranged basket.
4. Cook for 4 to 5 minutes, or until sautéed and cooked through.
5. Meanwhile, place the sugar in a shallow bowl. Spoon the jam into a baked good pack or a zip-top plastic sack with a corner cut off.
6. Brush the doughnuts with the liquefied spread and promptly dig every one in the sugar. Move to a plate or wire rack to cool for a couple minutes.
7. Using the finish of a wooden spoon, punch a hole in the side of every doughnut to make a pit for the jelly.
8. Carefully pipe the jam from the sack into the opening of every doughnut. Serve immediately.

Change It Up: Instead of filling the doughnuts with jam, take a stab at funneling in chocolate-hazelnut spread, Bavarian cream, or buttercream frosting.

Per serving (1 doughnut): Calories: 342; Total fat: 13g; Saturated fat: 6g; Cholesterol: 20mg; Sodium: 617mg; Carbohydrates: 54g; Fiber: 1g; Protein: 4g

FRENCH TOAST STICKS

FAMILY FAVORITE
VEGETARIAN

Serves 4/Prep Time: 10 minutes/Fry Time: 9 minutes

Since the times of the Roman Empire, individuals have been absorbing lifeless bread milk and browning it in oil or margarine. French toast sticks are the most recent craze.
Easily made in the air fryer, they keep end of the week breakfast fast and easy.

Oil, for splashing
6 enormous eggs
1⅓ cups milk
2 teaspoons vanilla extract
1 teaspoon ground cinnamon
8 cuts bread, cut into thirds
Syrup of decision, for serving

1. Preheat the air fryer to 370°F. Line the air fryer bin with material and splash softly with oil.
2. In a shallow bowl, whisk the eggs, milk, vanilla, and cinnamon.
3. Dunk one slice of bread in the egg blend, making a point to cover the two sides. Work rapidly so the bread doesn't get saturated. Quickly move the bread to the arranged basket.
4. Repeat with the leftover bread, ensuring the pieces don't contact one another. You might have to work in groups, contingent upon the size of your air fryer.
5. Cook for 5 minutes, flip, and cook for one more 3 to 4 minutes, until carmelized and crispy.
6. Serve promptly with your most loved syrup.

Change It Up: Instead of syrup, have a go at garnish the French toast sticks with new organic product or a tidying of confectioners' sugar and whipped cream, or dunk them in warmed chocolate-hazelnut spread, peanut butter, or caramel sauce.

Per serving: Calories: 326; Total fat: 12g; Saturated fat: 4g; Cholesterol: 287mg; Sodium: 333mg; Carbohydrates: 32g; Fiber: 4g; Protein: 20g

HOMEMADE TOASTER PASTRIES

FAMILY FAVORITE

Makes 6 baked goods/Prep Time: 10 minutes/Fry Time: 11 minutes

The toaster oven cake was presented in 1964. This adaptation can be served warm for breakfast, or you can pack the cooled baked goods in a lunch box.

Oil, for spraying
1 (15-ounce) bundle refrigerated piecrust 6 tablespoons jam or jelly of choice
2 cups confectioners' sugar
3 tablespoons milk
1 to 2 tablespoons sprinkles of choice

1. Preheat the air fryer to 350°F. Line the air fryer container with material and shower delicately with oil.
2. Cut the piecrust into 12 square shapes, around 3 by 4 inches each. You should reroll the mixture scraps to get 12 rectangles.
3. Spread 1 tablespoon of jam in the focal point of 6 square shapes, leaving ¼ inch around the edges.
4. Pour some water into a little bowl. Use your finger to saturate the edge of every square shape.
5. Top every square shape with one more and use your fingers to press around the edges. Utilizing the prongs of a fork, seal the edges of the mixture and punch a couple of holes in the highest point of every one. Place the cakes in the arranged basket.
6. Cook for 11 minutes. Let cool completely.
7. In a medium bowl, whisk together the confectioners' sugar and milk. Spread the icing over the highest points of the baked goods and add sprinkles. Serve immediately.

Change It Up: To make natively constructed piecrust, in an enormous bowl, consolidate 2½ cups universally handy flour, 1 teaspoon sugar, ½ teaspoon salt, 1 cup (2 sticks) cold margarine, and ½ cup ice water. Utilizing a baked good shaper or 2 sharp blades, work the fixings until the batter begins to arrange. Place the mixture on a
all around floured surface and utilize a moving pin to fold it into a 9-inch circle.

Per serving (1 baked good): Calories: 505; Total fat: 18g; Saturated fat: 7g; Cholesterol: 1mg; Sodium: 300mg; Carbohydrates: 83g; Fiber: 2g; Protein: 2g

CAN YOU FRY IT?

PANCAKES

You have to make pancakes one at a time. Prepare the batter according to the package instructions. Pour enough batter for one pancake on a greased air fryer–safe pan. Cook at 330°F for 5 to 7 minutes.

GLUTEN-FREE GRANOLA CEREAL

GLUTEN-FREE
VEGETARIAN

Makes 3½ cups/Prep Time: 7 minutes/Fry Time: 30 minutes

This granola cereal is not difficult to make, practical, and, IMHO, preferable tasting over comparable oats you can purchase. In the event that without gluten food sources are not a need for you, change out the oats for a grain you prefer.

Oil, for spraying
1½ cups without gluten rolled oats
½ cup hacked walnuts
½ cup cleaved almonds
½ cup pumpkin seeds
¼ cup maple syrup or honey
1 tablespoon toasted sesame oil or vegetable oil
1 teaspoon ground cinnamon
½ teaspoon salt
½ cup dried cranberries

1. Preheat the air fryer to 250°F. Line the air fryer bushel with material and shower gently with oil. (Try not to avoid the progression of covering the bin; the material will hold the granola back from falling

through the holes.)
2. In a huge bowl, combine as one the oats, pecans, almonds, pumpkin seeds, maple syrup, sesame oil, cinnamon, and salt.
3. Spread the combination in an even layer in the arranged basket.
4. Cook for 30 minutes, mixing each 10 minutes.
5. Transfer the granola to a bowl, add the dried cranberries, and throw to combine.
6. Let cool to room temperature prior to putting away in an impenetrable container.

Change It Up: Change up the flavors by adding dried blueberries, dried strawberries, dried pineapple, smaller than expected chocolate chips, scaled down M&Ms, or chipped coconut.

Per serving (½ cup): Calories: 287; Total fat: 17g; Saturated fat: 2g; Cholesterol: 0mg; Sodium: 190mg; Carbohydrates: 30g; Fiber: 5g; Protein: 8g

GLUTEN-FREE CINNAMON-RAISIN GRANOLA BARS

GLUTEN-FREE
VEGETARIAN

Makes 6 bars or 12 squares/Prep Time: 5 minutes/Fry Time: 15 minutes

Granola bars are a nibble time staple and are incredible for throwing in lunch boxes, sports packs, storage spaces, and excursion crates. You can make this variant with without gluten or customary oats.

Oil, for spraying
1¼ cups sans gluten moved oats, divided
¼ cup pressed light earthy colored sugar 1 teaspoon ground cinnamon
8 tablespoons (1 stick) unsalted margarine, dissolved 3 tablespoons honey
1 tablespoon vegetable oil
1 teaspoon vanilla concentrate 2 tablespoons raisins

1. Line an air fryer-safe baking dish with material and shower daintily with oil.
2. In a blender, beat about portion of the oats until smooth. Move to a medium bowl. Add the excess oats, earthy colored sugar, and cinnamon and mix to combine.
3. Add the margarine, honey, vegetable oil, and vanilla and mix to consolidate. Overlap in the raisins.
4. Transfer the combination to the pre-arranged dish and press into an even layer.
5. Cook at 320°F for 10 minutes. Increment the hotness to 360°F and cook for another 5 minutes.
6. Let cool to room temperature, then, at that point, freeze prior to cutting into bars and serving.

Change It Up: Add dried organic product, smaller than usual chocolate chips, or coconut drops to give the granola bars more variety.

Per serving (1 bar/2 squares): Calories: 299; Total fat: 19g; Saturated fat: 10g; Cholesterol: 41mg; Sodium: 125mg; Carbohydrates: 32g; Fiber: 2g; Protein: 3g

CINNAMON-RAISIN BAGELS

VEGETARIAN

Makes 4 bagels/Prep Time: 30 minutes/Fry Time: 10 minutes

Bagels started in Jewish people group in Poland during the 1600s. Customarily, they are produced using a yeasted mixture that is bubbled and afterward heated, giving them their thick surface and chewy outside. This rendition cuts your planning time by utilizing self-rising flour.

Oil, for spraying
¼ cup raisins
1 cup self-rising flour, in addition to additional for tidying 1 cup plain Greek yogurt
1 teaspoon ground cinnamon
1 huge egg

1. Line the air fryer bin with material and shower delicately with oil.
2. Place the raisins in a bowl of heated water and let sit for 10 to 15 minutes, until they have plumped. This will make them extra juicy.
3. In an enormous bowl, combine as one the flour, yogurt, and cinnamon with your hands or a huge silicone spatula until a ball is framed. It will be very tacky for a while.
4. Drain the raisins and delicately work them into the wad of dough.
5. Place the batter on a softly floured work surface and separation into 4 equivalent pieces. Fold each piece into a 8-or 9-inch-long rope and shape it into a circle, squeezing the closures together to seal.
6. In a little bowl, whisk the egg. Brush the egg onto the highest points of the dough.
7. Place the batter in the arranged basket.
8. Cook at 350°F for 10 minutes. Serve immediately.

Change It Up: To make everything bagels, sprinkle each round of dough with 2 teaspoons everything bagel seasoning (see Fry Fact) after brushing with the egg. To make onion bagels, sprinkle each round of batter with ¼ teaspoon onion powder and ½ teaspoon dried minced onion drops in the wake of brushing with the egg. Cook as instructed.

Per serving (1 bagel): Calories: 198; Total fat: 4g; Saturated fat: 2g; Cholesterol: 54mg; Sodium: 420mg; Carbohydrates: 35g; Fiber: 2g; Protein: 7g

BANANA-NUT MUFFINS

FAMILY FAVORITE
VEGETARIAN

Makes 10 biscuits/Prep Time: 5 minutes/Fry Time: 15 minutes

Bananas are easy decisions for smoothies, cereal, cakes, pies, breads, thus considerably more. They assist with restricting fixings together, yet in addition go about as a sugar, so you can diminish how much sugar in a recipe.

Oil, for spraying
2 extremely ready bananas
½ cup stuffed light brown sugar
⅓ cup canola oil or vegetable oil
1 enormous egg
1 teaspoon vanilla extract
¾ cup generally useful flour
1 teaspoon baking powder
1 teaspoon ground cinnamon
½ cup hacked walnuts

1. Preheat the air fryer to 320°F. Shower 10 silicone biscuit cups gently with oil.
2. In a medium bowl, crush the bananas. Add the earthy colored sugar, canola oil, egg, and vanilla and mix to combine.
3. Fold in the flour, baking powder, and cinnamon until just combined.
4. Add the pecans and crease a couple of times to convey all through the batter.
5. Divide the hitter similarly among the pre-arranged biscuit cups and spot them in the bushel. You might have to work in clumps, contingent upon the size of your air fryer.
6. Cook for 15 minutes, or until brilliant brown and a toothpick embedded into the focal point of a biscuit tells the truth. The air fryer will in general brown biscuits more than the stove, so don't be frightened on the off chance that they are more obscure than you're utilized to. They will in any case taste great.
7. Let cool on a wire rack before serving.

Change It Up: Try these biscuits with hacked walnuts, macadamia nuts, white or semisweet chocolate chips, or even cleaved dates.

Per serving (1 biscuit): Calories: 208; Total fat: 12g; Saturated fat: 1g; Cholesterol: 19mg; Sodium: 11mg; Carbohydrates: 25g; Fiber: 1g; Protein: 3g

CHEESY SCRAMBLED EGGS

GLUTEN-FREE
SUPER-FAST
VEGETARIAN

Serves 2/Prep Time: 2 minutes/Fry Time: 9 minutes

Staples like fried eggs have been around for quite a long time, and it's no big surprise they pair well with pretty much everything. You can have these fleecy, messy eggs on the morning meal table in under 15 minutes. Pair them with Jelly Donuts or Breakfast Hash.

1 teaspoon unsalted spread
2 enormous eggs
2 tablespoons milk
2 tablespoons destroyed cheddar Salt
Freshly ground dark pepper

1. Preheat the air fryer to 300°F. Place the spread in an air fryer-safe skillet and cook for 1 to 2 minutes, until melted.
2. In a little bowl, whisk together the eggs, milk, and cheddar. Season with salt and dark pepper. Move the combination to the pan.
3. Cook for 3 minutes. Mix the eggs and push them toward the focal point of the pan.
4. Cook for an additional 2 minutes, then, at that point, mix once more. Cook for an additional 2 minutes, until the eggs are recently cooked. Serve warm.

Fry Fact: The eggs will keep on concocting for to 3 minutes after they have been taken out from the hotness, so be mindful so as not to overcook.

Per serving: Calories: 127; Total fat: 10g; Saturated fat: 4g; Cholesterol: 200mg; Sodium: 217mg; Carbohydrates: 1g; Fiber: 0g; Protein: 9g

HARD-BOILED EGGS

GLUTEN-FREE
VEGETARIAN

Makes 6 eggs/Prep Time: 3 minutes/Fry Time: 15 minutes

When I was first living all alone, I asked my loved ones for hard-bubbled egg plans, and every individual sent me an alternate one. Yet, presently I have this rendition, which doesn't need bubbling water. It's simple and basically foolproof.

Oil, for showering 6 huge eggs

1. Preheat the air fryer to 270°F. Fill a bowl with water and ice. Line the air fryer bin with material and shower daintily with oil.
2. Place the eggs in the arranged basket.
3. Cook for 15 minutes.
4. Using utensils, move the eggs to the bowl of ice water to prevent them from cooking. Let sit for around 1 moment, or until adequately cool to handle.
5. Pat dry the eggs with a paper towel or a kitchen towel and serve or use quickly, or refrigerate for up to 7 days.

Change It Up: For delicate bubbled eggs, cook for 10 minutes. For medium-bubbled eggs, cook for 12 minutes.

Per serving (1 egg): Calories: 72; Total fat: 5g; Saturated fat: 2g; Cholesterol: 186mg; Sodium: 71mg; Carbohydrates: 0g; Fiber: 0g; Protein: 6g

CAN YOU FRY IT?

BREAKFAST BURRITO

Burritos are a great way to use leftovers. Line the air fryer basket with parchment and spray lightly with oil. In a large bowl, combine the cooked filling ingredients of your choice. Place about ½ cup of the mixture on a large flour tortilla. Fold in the sides and roll to close. Place the burrito in the prepared basket, spray lightly with oil, and cook at 330°F for 5 to 8 minutes, until heated through.

PUFFED EGG TARTS

FAMILY FAVORITE
VEGETARIAN

Makes 4 tarts/Prep Time: 10 minutes/Fry Time: 42 minutes

From the start, these tarts give off an impression of being a mixture of Yorkshire pudding and its American cousin, egg-in-a-opening. Once more they are made of puffed baked good air singed and afterward squeezed into "cups," loaded up with an egg, and seared. The outcomes are adequately great to serve for Sunday brunch.

Oil, for spraying
All-reason flour, for dusting
1 (12-ounce) sheet frozen puff cake, thawed
¾ cup destroyed cheddar, isolated 4
enormous eggs
2 teaspoons slashed new parsley
Salt
Freshly ground dark pepper

1. Preheat the air fryer to 390°F. Line the air fryer bushel with material and splash daintily with oil.
2. Lightly dust your work surface with flour. Unfurl the puff cake and cut it into 4 equivalent squares. Place 2 squares in the arranged basket.
3. Cook for 10 minutes.
4. Remove the bin. Press the focal point of every tart shell with a spoon to make an indentation.
5. Sprinkle 3 tablespoons of cheddar into every space and break 1 egg into the focal point of every tart shell.
6. Cook for one more 7 to 11 minutes, or until the eggs are cooked to your ideal doneness.
7. Repeat with the excess puff cake squares, cheddar, and eggs.
8. Sprinkle equitably with the parsley, and season with salt and dark pepper. Serve immediately.

Fry Fact: For the best outcomes, break each egg into a little dish, then, at that point, cautiously slide it onto the puffed tart as opposed to attempting to break the egg over the tart.

Per serving (1 tart): Calories: 634; Total fat: 44g; Saturated fat: 14g; Cholesterol: 208mg; Sodium: 420mg; Carbohydrates: 41g; Fiber: 1g; Protein: 18g

EASY HASH BROWNS

FAMILY FAVORITE
VEGETARIAN

Serves 4/Prep Time: 10 minutes, in addition to 20 minutes to splash/Fry Time: 20 minutes

Crispy hash earthy colored potatoes are a cherished breakfast side dish, and you don't need to visit the neighborhood burger joint to get them. Turn this recipe into a meal by topping the hash browns with a fried egg or serving them as a side to <u>Cheesy Scrambled Eggs</u>. They're scrumptious with a bit of ketchup.

Oil, for splashing
3 chestnut
potatoes
2 tablespoons minced onion
1 teaspoon granulated garlic
½ teaspoon salt
¼ teaspoon newly ground dark pepper 2
teaspoons olive oil

1. Line the air fryer bin with material and shower daintily with oil.
2. Peel the potatoes and mesh them against the biggest openings on a container grater. Move the ground potatoes to a bowl of cold water and let douse for around 20 minutes, which will eliminate a portion of the starch and give you crunchier results.
3. Drain the potatoes, place them on a few pieces of paper towels, roll them up, and crush out as much water as possible.
4. Transfer the potatoes to an enormous bowl. Add the onion, garlic, salt, dark pepper, and olive oil and blend well.
5. Spread the potato combination in an even layer in the arranged basket.
6. Cook at 400°F for 10 minutes, shake, and cook for an additional 10 minutes, until seared and crispy.
7. Let cool for 2 to 4 minutes before serving.

Faster Frying: To make this formula considerably quicker, utilize frozen destroyed hash earthy colors. Defrost them completely prior to throwing with different fixings and cooking.

Per serving: Calories: 242; Total fat: 2g; Saturated fat: 0g; Cholesterol: 0mg; Sodium: 305mg; Carbohydrates: 51g; Fiber: 4g; Protein: 6g

BREAKFAST HASH

FAMILY FAVORITE
VEGETARIAN

Serves 6/Prep Time: 10 minutes/Fry Time: 30 minutes

Breakfast hash began as a method for spending extras. This variant contains onion and chime pepper, however go ahead and add different vegetables, similar to broccoli or asparagus. The dish makes an extraordinary lunch or supper when presented with toast, hollandaise sauce, or even heated beans. Give it with a singed egg a shot top and a side of bacon or sausage.

Oil, for spraying
3 medium chestnut potatoes, diced
½ yellow onion, diced
1 green ringer pepper, cultivated and
diced 2 tablespoons olive oil
2 teaspoons granulated garlic
1 teaspoon salt
½ teaspoon newly ground dark pepper

1. Line the air fryer container with material and splash softly with oil.
2. In a huge bowl, combine as one the potatoes, onion, chime pepper, and olive oil.
3. Add the garlic, salt, and dark pepper and mix until equally coated.
4. Transfer the combination to the arranged basket.
5. Cook at 400°F for 20 to 30 minutes, shaking or mixing at regular intervals, until carmelized and firm. On the off chance that you shower the potatoes with a little oil each time you mix, they will settle the score crispier.

Pair It With: This hash is great with Cheesy Scrambled Eggs or Puffed Egg Tarts.

Per serving: Calories: 133; Total fat: 5g; Saturated fat: 1g; Cholesterol: 0mg; Sodium: 394mg; Carbohydrates: 21g; Fiber: 2g; Protein: 3g

HAM AND CHEESE CRESCENTS

SUPER-FAST

Makes 8 rolls/Prep Time: 5 minutes/Fry Time: 7 minutes

This rapid breakfast is made with refrigerated bow roll batter. Assuming you are enjoying nature in a movement trailer, make these bows to fuel your open air adventures.

Oil, for spraying
1 (8-ounce) can refrigerated bow rolls 4 cuts store ham
8 cuts American cheese
2 tablespoons unsalted spread, melted

1. Line the air fryer bushel with material and splash daintily with oil.
2. Separate the batter into 8 pieces.
3. Tear the ham cuts fifty-fifty and spot 1 piece on each piece of mixture. Top each with 1 cut of cheese.
4. Roll up each piece of batter, beginning the more extensive side.
5. Place the rolls in the pre-arranged bin. Brush with the softened butter.
6. Cook at 320°F for 6 to 7 minutes, or until puffed and brilliant brown and the cheddar is melted.

Fry Fact: Individually wrapped cheddar cuts liquefy better compared to cuts off a square of cheddar and give the dish an in general creamier texture.

Per serving (1 roll): Calories: 249; Total fat: 17g; Saturated fat: 8g; Cholesterol: 44mg; Sodium: 640mg; Carbohydrates: 14g; Fiber: 0g; Protein: 11g

"ALL THE FAVORITES" QUICHE

FAMILY FAVORITE

Serves 6/Prep Time: 10 minutes/Fry Time: 19 minutes

Quiche is an extraordinarily flexible breakfast and early lunch most loved on the grounds that you can change it up of fixings. This formula joins the most well known quiche fixings, including spinach, ham, bacon, and cheddar cheese.

Oil, for

showering 6 huge
eggs
½ cup milk
½ cup harsh cream
½ cup slashed child spinach
¼ cup diced ham
1 tablespoon minced onion
¼ cup diced tomato
2 tablespoons bacon bits
1 tablespoon hacked new chives
1 cup destroyed cheddar, separated 1 (9-
inch) frozen piecrust, thawed

1. Line the air fryer bushel with material and splash delicately with oil.
2. In a medium bowl, combine as one the eggs, milk, acrid cream, spinach, ham, onion, tomato, bacon bits, and chives.
3. Sprinkle half of the cheddar in the lower part of the piecrust. Pour the egg combination over the cheese.
4. Place the quiche in the arranged basket.
5. Cook at 300°F for 12 minutes. Sprinkle the excess cheddar over the top and cook for one more 5 to 7 minutes, or until the middle is set and the top is brilliant brown.
6. Let rest for 5 minutes prior to cutting into cuts and serving.

Fry Fact: The quiche is set when it no longer shakes in the center. Assuming the top is searing excessively fast, tent it with aluminum foil for the leftover cooking time.

Per serving: Calories: 330; Total fat: 24g; Saturated fat: 9g; Cholesterol: 223mg; Sodium: 510mg; Carbohydrates: 14g; Fiber: 1g; Protein: 16g

CHAPTER 3
SNACKS AND APPETIZERS

Cinnamon-Apple Chips Spicy
Ranch Oyster Snack Crackers
Potato Chips Fried
Parsnips
Spiced Chickpeas
Garlic-Parmesan Croutons
Jalapeño Peppers
Mozzarella Balls Fried
Artichoke Hearts
Wontons Asiago
Shishito Peppers
Buffalo Chicken French Bread Pizza Loaded
Tater Tot Skewers Soft
Bites with Honey Mustard Dip Vegetable Fry
Nachos
Bacon-Wrapped Sausages
Thai-Inspired Sweet Chili Cauliflower

FRIED ARTICHOKE HEARTS

CINNAMON-APPLE CHIPS

GLUTEN-FREE
VEGETARIAN

Serves 4/Prep Time: 10 minutes/Fry Time: 32 minutes

Dried apple chips are a solid option in contrast to oily prepackaged bites like potato chips. Locally acquired forms regularly incorporate a ton of additives, yet this formula doesn't need a dehydrator-or a lot of your time.

Oil, for spraying
2 Red Delicious or Honeycrisp apples
¼ teaspoon ground cinnamon, divided

1. Line the air fryer bushel with material and splash softly with oil.
2. Trim the lopsided finishes off the apples. Utilizing a mandoline on the most slender setting or a sharp blade, cut the apples into exceptionally dainty cuts. Dispose of the cores.
3. Place half of the apple cuts in a solitary layer in the pre-arranged bin and sprinkle with half of the cinnamon.
4. Place a metal air fryer trivet on top of the apples to hold them back from zooming around while they are cooking.
5. Cook at 300°F for 16 minutes, flipping like clockwork to guarantee in any event, cooking. Rehash with the excess apple cuts and cinnamon.
6. Let cool to room temperature prior to serving. The chips will solidify as they cool.

Change It Up: To make apple nachos for an extraordinary sweet, heap the apple chips on a plate and sprinkle them with chocolate or caramel sauce. Top with sprinkles, smaller than normal chocolate confections, and slashed nuts.

Per serving: Calories: 31; Total fat: 0g; Saturated fat: 0g; Cholesterol: 0mg; Sodium: 1mg; Carbohydrates: 8g; Fiber: 1g; Protein: 0g

SPICY RANCH OYSTER SNACK CRACKERS

SUPER-FAST
VEGETARIAN

Serves 6/Prep Time: 3 minutes/Fry Time: 12 minutes

Party nibble blends have been around since the 1950s, when boxed grain makers attempted to get customers to serve cereal past breakfast. This wind on the exemplary is made with clam wafers. These wafers are not difficult to make and will remain new for the term of a party.

Oil, for spraying
¼ cup olive oil
2 teaspoons dry farm preparing
1 teaspoon stew powder
½ teaspoon dried dill
½ teaspoon granulated garlic
½ teaspoon salt
1 (9-ounce) sack shellfish crackers

1. Preheat the air fryer to 325°F. Line the air fryer bushel with material and shower softly with oil.
2. In an enormous bowl, combine as one the olive oil, farm preparing, stew powder, dill, garlic, and salt. Add the wafers and throw until equitably coated.
3. Place the combination in the arranged basket.
4. Cook for 10 to 12 minutes, shaking or blending each 3 to 4 minutes, or until fresh and brilliant brown.

Change It Up: For a more conventional bite blend flavor, in a huge bowl, combine as one ¼ cup oil, ¼ cup Worcestershire sauce, 1 tablespoon lemon juice, 1 teaspoon garlic powder, ½ teaspoon onion powder, ½ teaspoon celery salt, and ½ teaspoon prepared salt and throw with the shellfish saltines before cooking.

Per serving: Calories: 260; Total fat: 13g; Saturated fat: 2g; Cholesterol: 0mg; Sodium: 607mg; Carbohydrates: 32g; Fiber: 1g; Protein: 4g

SEA SALT POTATO CHIPS

GLUTEN-FREE
VEGETARIAN

Serves 4/Prep Time: 15 minutes, in addition to 20 minutes to douse/Fry Time: 27 minutes

At times straightforward adaptations of your cherished bites, similar to potato chips, are what the air fryer does best. These air-seared chips are a lot of lower in fat and sodium and won't leave your fingers canvassed in

grease.

Oil, for spraying
4 medium yellow potatoes
1 tablespoon oil
⅛ to ¼ teaspoon fine ocean salt

1. Line the air fryer crate with material and splash gently with oil.
2. Using a mandoline or an exceptionally sharp blade, cut the potatoes into extremely dainty slices.
3. Place the cuts in a bowl of cold water and let douse for around 20 minutes.
4. Drain the potatoes, move them to a plate fixed with paper towels, and pat dry.
5. Drizzle the oil over the potatoes, sprinkle with the salt, and throw to consolidate. Move to the arranged basket.
6. Cook at 200°F for 20 minutes. Throw the chips, increment the hotness to 400°F, and cook for one more 5 to 7 minutes, until crispy.

Change It Up: Add your cherished flavors by showering with 1 to 2 teaspoons vinegar, sprinkling with powdered popcorn cheddar enhancing, or adding farm, onion, or taco seasoning.

Per serving: Calories: 195; Total fat: 4g; Saturated fat: 0g; Cholesterol: 0mg; Sodium: 158mg; Carbohydrates: 37g; Fiber: 5g; Protein: 4g

FRIED PICKLE CHIPS

VEGETARIAN

Serves 4/Prep Time: 20 minutes, in addition to 1 hour to douse/Fry Time: 12 minutes

While singed pickles are a typical nibble in the South, the first realized printed formula showed up in Quite a while's Oakland Tribune during the 1960s. (They were promoted with regards to a year after the fact in Arkansas.) If you are staying away from gluten, use without gluten flour and bread pieces. These chips are compelling presented with Cajun plunging sauce or farm dressing.

Oil, for spraying
2 cups cut dill or sweet pickles, depleted 1
cup buttermilk

2 cups generally useful
flour 2 huge eggs,
beaten
2 cups panko bread crumbs
¼ teaspoon salt

1. Line the air fryer container with material and shower gently with oil.
2. In a shallow bowl, consolidate the pickles and buttermilk and let drench for somewhere around 60 minutes, then, at that point, drain.
3. Place the flour, beaten eggs, and bread morsels in isolated bowls.
4. Coat each pickle chip daintily in the flour, dunk in the eggs, and dig in the bread scraps. Be certain every one is equitably coated.
5. Place the pickle contributes the pre-arranged container, sprinkle with the salt, and splash daintily with oil. You might have to work in clumps, contingent upon the size of your air fryer.
6. Cook at 390°F for 5 minutes, flip, and cook for one more 5 to 7 minutes, or until firm. Serve hot.

Fry Fact: If you don't have buttermilk close by, put 1 tablespoon white vinegar in an estimating cup and add milk to the 1-cup mark. Let sit for around 5 minutes before using.

Per serving: Calories: 330; Total fat: 6g; Saturated fat: 1g; Cholesterol: 64mg; Sodium: 564mg; Carbohydrates: 58g; Fiber: 2g; Protein: 10g

TACO-SPICED CHICKPEAS

GLUTEN-FREE
VEGETARIAN

Serves 3/Prep Time: 5 minutes/Fry Time: 17 minutes

Chickpeas, likewise called garbanzo beans, have acquired ubiquity as a sound tidbit, especially when prepared and broiled. They're loaded with protein and fiber, and the air fryer gives them a wonderful crunch.

Oil, for spraying
1 (15½-ounce) can chickpeas, depleted
1 teaspoon bean stew powder
½ teaspoon ground cumin
½ teaspoon salt
½ teaspoon granulated garlic
2 teaspoons lime juice

1. Line the air fryer container with material and shower daintily with oil. Place the chickpeas in the arranged basket.
2. Cook at 390°F for 17 minutes, shaking or mixing the chickpeas and showering softly with oil each 5 to 7 minutes.
3. In a little bowl, combine as one the bean stew powder, cumin, salt, and garlic.
4. When 2 to 3 minutes of cooking time remain, sprinkle half of the flavoring blend over the chickpeas. Finish cooking.
5. Transfer the chickpeas to a medium bowl and throw with the leftover flavoring blend and the lime juice. Serve immediately.

Change It Up: There are endless choices for elective flavor blends. Sprinkle the chickpeas with salt and newly ground dark pepper or some dry farm preparing. Attempt a grill style by combining as one 1½ teaspoons paprika, 1 teaspoon stuffed light earthy colored sugar, ½ teaspoon granulated garlic, ½ teaspoon dry mustard, and ¼ teaspoon newly ground dark pepper and sprinkling over the chickpeas not long prior to serving. Make a sweet assortment by blending 1 tablespoon granulated sugar and ½ teaspoon ground cinnamon and preparing with the chickpeas.

Per serving: Calories: 151; Total fat: 7g; Saturated fat: 1g; Cholesterol: 0mg; Sodium: 576mg; Carbohydrates: 19g; Fiber: 5g; Protein: 6g

GARLIC-PARMESAN CROUTONS

SUPER-FAST
VEGETARIAN

Serves 4/Prep Time: 3 minutes/Fry Time: 12 minutes

A plate of mixed greens isn't a plate of mixed greens except if it incorporates bread garnishes. Making your own is an incredible method for spending flat bread or the extra heels you can't exactly bear to discard. A couple of day-old bread works truly well.

Oil, for spraying
4 cups cubed French bread
1 tablespoon ground Parmesan cheddar 3 tablespoons olive oil
1 tablespoon granulated garlic
½ teaspoon unsalted salt

1. Line the air fryer bin with material and shower gently with oil.

2. In a huge bowl, combine as one the bread, Parmesan cheddar, olive oil, garlic, and salt, throwing with your hands to uniformly disperse the flavors. Move the covered bread solid shapes to the arranged basket.
3. Cook at 350°F for 10 to 12 minutes, mixing once following 5 minutes, or until fresh and brilliant brown.

Change It Up: These bread garnishes are an incredible method for spending miscellaneous items of extra bread-attempt bagels, sandwich bread, or pumpernickel bread.

Per serving: Calories: 277; Total fat: 12g; Saturated fat: 2g; Cholesterol: 1mg; Sodium: 600mg; Carbohydrates: 35g; Fiber: 2g; Protein: 8g

CAN YOU FRY IT?

QUESADILLAS

Line the air fryer basket with parchment and spray lightly with oil. Lay out a large flour tortilla and cover with shredded cheddar cheese. Top with another tortilla. Place in the prepared basket. Cook at 400°F for 5 minutes, flip, and cook for another 3 to 5 minutes, or until golden brown and the cheese is melted.

JALAPEÑO POPPERS

FAMILY FAVORITE
GLUTEN-FREE
VEGETARIAN

Serves 4/Prep Time: 10 minutes/Fry Time: 20 minutes

An Americanized adaptation of chiles rellenos, a conventional Mexican dish, poppers join gentle jalapeño chiles, cheddar, and pureed tomatoes. This formula is made with sans gluten bread morsels, yet you can utilize normal. To make it veggie lover, use sans dairy cream cheese.

Oil, for spraying
8 ounces cream cheese
¾ cup without gluten bread pieces, isolated 2 tablespoons hacked new parsley
½ teaspoon granulated garlic
½ teaspoon salt
10 jalapeño peppers, split and seeded

1. Line the air fryer bin with material and shower gently with oil.
2. In a medium bowl, combine as one the cream cheddar, a big part of the bread scraps, the parsley, garlic, and salt.
3. Spoon the blend into the jalapeño parts. Tenderly press the stuffed jalapeños in the leftover bread crumbs.
4. Place the stuffed jalapeños in the arranged basket.
5. Cook at 370°F for 20 minutes, or until the cheddar is liquefied and the bread pieces are fresh and brilliant brown.

Fry Fact: Remove every one of the seeds and the white layer of the jalapeños, except if you like to keep things on the more blazing side. It's smart to wear gloves when taking care of peppers so you don't chance getting buildup in your eyes or on whatever else you touch.

Per serving: Calories: 286; Total fat: 21g; Saturated fat: 11g; Cholesterol: 62mg; Sodium: 648mg; Carbohydrates: 20g; Fiber: 2g; Protein: 7g

MOZZARELLA BALLS

FAMILY FAVORITE
VEGETARIAN

Makes 15 to 20 balls/Prep Time: 20 minutes, in addition to 1½ hours to freeze/Fry Time: 5

minutes

Making my own singed mozzarella was at the first spot on my list when I got my first air fryer. Serve these balls with marinara sauce, hot sauce, farm dressing, or even a Southern fry sauce for dipping.

1 (8-ounce) bundle scaled down mozzarella balls or 4 to 5 mozzarella cheddar sticks cut into scaled down pieces
1 huge egg
¼ cup bread crumbs
¼ cup panko bread crumbs
½ teaspoon onion powder
½ teaspoon garlic powder
½ teaspoon salt
¼ cup universally handy flour Oil, for spraying

1. Line a baking sheet with material paper.
2. Put the mozzarella balls in a zip-top plastic pack, seal, and spot in the cooler for something like 30 minutes.
3. In a shallow bowl, whisk the egg and set aside.
4. In another shallow bowl, combine as one the bread scraps, panko bread morsels, onion powder, garlic powder, and salt.
5. Place the frozen mozzarella balls and the flour in another zip-top plastic sack, seal, and shake well to cover the balls with flour.
6. Dip every mozzarella ball in the egg, then, at that point, dig in the bread morsel combination. Move to the pre-arranged baking sheet.
7. Place the baking sheet in the cooler for somewhere around 1 hour.
8. Preheat the air fryer to 370°F. Line the air fryer bushel with material and shower gently with oil.
9. Transfer the mozzarella balls to the pre-arranged bin. You might have to work in bunches, contingent upon the size of your air fryer. Splash gently with oil.
10. Cook for 5 minutes, or until brilliant brown and crispy.

Pair It With: These mozzarella balls are great on a game-day party platter with Sea Salt Potato Chips and Fried Pickle Chips.

Per serving (5 balls): Calories: 289; Total fat: 18g; Saturated fat: 8g; Cholesterol: 91mg; Sodium: 739mg; Carbohydrates: 15g; Fiber: 1g; Protein: 16g

FRIED ARTICHOKE HEARTS

VEGETARIAN

Serves 10/Prep Time: 10 minutes/Fry Time: 12 minutes

Recipes for singed artichokes started in the sixteenth century in Roman Jewish cooking. Today they are a famous starter. The firm panko coats the delicate, delicious artichoke and makes a heavenly combination.

Oil, for spraying
3 (14-ounce) jars quartered artichokes, depleted and tapped dry
½ cup mayonnaise
1 cup panko bread crumbs
⅓ cup ground Parmesan
cheddar Salt
Freshly ground dark pepper

1. Line the air fryer bin with material and shower gently with oil.
2. Place the artichokes on a plate. Put the mayonnaise and bread scraps in isolated bowls.
3. Working each in turn, dig every artichoke piece in the mayonnaise, then, at that point, in the bread morsels to cover.
4. Place the artichokes in the pre-arranged crate. You might have to work in bunches, contingent upon the size of your air fryer.
5. Cook at 370°F for 10 to 12 minutes, or until fresh and brilliant brown.
6. Sprinkle with the Parmesan cheddar and season with salt and dark pepper. Serve immediately.

Faster Frying: Try putting the bread pieces in a zip-top plastic sack, adding numerous mayonnaise-shrouded artichoke hearts, and shaking delicately to coat.

Per serving: Calories: 160; Total fat: 10g; Saturated fat: 2g; Cholesterol: 7mg; Sodium: 241mg; Carbohydrates: 16g; Fiber: 8g; Protein: 4g

CREAM CHEESE WONTONS

VEGETARIAN

Makes 20 wontons/Prep Time: 15 minutes/Fry Time: 6 minutes

Wontons are usually steamed or bubbled and served in soup, yet southern style variants are appearing on an ever increasing number of menus. This variant has a firm external covering with dissolved cream cheddar within. Have a go at dunking them in prepared sauce or a tart teriyaki sauce.

Oil, for spraying
20 wonton wrappers
4 ounces cream cheese

1. Line the air fryer bushel with material and shower delicately with oil.
2. Pour some water in a little bowl.
3. Lay out a wonton covering and spot 1 teaspoon of cream cheddar in the center.
4. Dip your finger in the water and dampen the edge of the wonton covering. Crease over the contrary corners to make a triangle and press the edges together.
5. Pinch the edges of the triangle together to frame an exemplary wonton shape. Place the wonton in the pre-arranged crate. Rehash with the leftover coverings and cream cheddar. You might have to work in clumps, contingent upon the size of your air fryer.
6. Cook at 400°F for 6 minutes, or until brilliant brown around the edges.

Change It Up: Try adding 1½ cups hacked child spinach, ½ cup seared ground wiener, or much extra destroyed chicken or dish meat to the filling.

Per serving (4 wontons): Calories: 171; Total fat: 8g; Saturated fat: 4g; Cholesterol: 28mg; Sodium: 266mg; Carbohydrates: 19g; Fiber: 1g; Protein: 4g

ASIAGO SHISHITO PEPPERS

GLUTEN-FREE
VEGETARIAN

Serves 4/Prep Time: 5 minutes/Fry Time: 10 minutes

Blistering shishito peppers draws out their flavor, particularly when matched with Asiago cheddar. Watch out: While these peppers are known for being gentle, around 1 out of 10 arrives at the higher reach on the hotness scale.

Oil, for spraying
6 ounces (around 12) shishito peppers 1 tablespoon olive oil
½ teaspoon salt
½ teaspoon lemon pepper
⅓ cup ground Asiago cheddar, divided

1. Line the air fryer container with material and splash softly with oil.
2. Rinse the shishitos and wipe off with paper towels.
3. In a huge bowl, combine as one the shishitos, olive oil, salt, and lemon pepper. Place the shishitos in the arranged basket.
4. Cook at 350°F for 10 minutes, or until rankled yet not burned.
5. Sprinkle with half of the cheddar and cook for 1 more minute.
6. Transfer to a serving plate. Quickly sprinkle with the leftover cheddar and serve.

Change It Up: Want to chance significantly more zest? Add 2 teaspoons sriracha to the mixture.

Per serving: Calories: 81; Total fat: 6g; Saturated fat: 2g; Cholesterol: 7mg; Sodium: 443mg; Carbohydrates: 5g; Fiber: 1g; Protein: 3g

BUFFALO CHICKEN FRENCH BREAD PIZZA

FAMILY FAVORITE

Serves 8/Prep Time: 10 minutes/Fry Time: 12 minutes

A tart blend of margarine and hot sauce, hot sauce is generally renowned for being slathered on chicken wings and combined with celery, carrots, and blue cheddar dressing. This formula changes everything around by spreading a chicken-and-cheddar combination on French bread.

Oil, for spraying
1 portion French bread, cut down the middle and split the long way 4 tablespoons unsalted margarine, melted
2 cups destroyed or diced rotisserie chicken
4 ounces cream cheese
3 tablespoons hot sauce, in addition to additional

for serving 2 tablespoons dry farm seasoning
2 cups destroyed mozzarella cheese
⅓ cup disintegrated blue cheese

1. Line the air fryer bin with material and splash softly with oil.
2. Brush the cut sides of the bread with the liquefied spread. Place the bread in the pre-arranged container. You might have to work in clusters, contingent upon the size of your air fryer.
3. Cook at 400°F for 5 to 7 minutes, or until the bread is toasted.
4. In a medium bowl, combine as one the chicken, cream cheddar, hot sauce, and farm seasoning.
5. Divide the combination similarly among the toasted bread and spread in an even layer.
6. Top with the mozzarella cheddar and blue cheddar and cook for one more 3 to 5 minutes, or until the cheddar is melted.
7. Let cool for 2 to 3 minutes prior to cutting into 2-inch cuts. Serve with extra hot sauce for drizzling.

Change It Up: For a more customary pizza flavor, spoon pizza sauce on top of the bread and top with 1 cup destroyed mozzarella cheddar, ¼ cup pepperoni cuts, and 2 teaspoons granulated garlic.

Per serving: Calories: 403; Total fat: 24g; Saturated fat: 13g; Cholesterol: 88mg; Sodium: 1066mg; Carbohydrates: 23g; Fiber: 1g; Protein: 23g

LOADED TATER TOT SKEWERS

FAMILY FAVORITE

Serves 6/Prep Time: 15 minutes/Fry Time: 20 minutes

These good potato toddler sticks are suggestive of amusement park snacks. Present with a farm plunge for an additional a piece of extravagance. You will require 6 metal sticks; ensure they fit in your air fryer.

Oil, for spraying
1 (20-ounce) pack frozen potato tots
½ cup destroyed cheddar cheese
½ cup bacon bits
½ teaspoon granulated garlic
2 tablespoons slashed new chives, for garnish

1. Preheat the air fryer to 400°F. Line the air fryer container with material and shower gently with oil.
2. Place the potato children in the pre-arranged bushel. They should cover the base with a couple of extra on top. You might have to work in bunches, contingent upon the size of your air fryer.
3. Cook for 15 minutes, shaking after 7 or 8 minutes.
4. Let cool just until you can deal with them. String 5 or 6 children on each skewer.
5. Place the sticks in the air fryer, sprinkle with the cheddar, bacon pieces, and garlic, and cook for an additional 5 minutes, until brilliant brown and crispy.
6. Sprinkle with the chives and serve.

Fry Fact: The toddlers are done when they are firm, crunchy, and brilliant brown outwardly. Recall that plans made in the air fryer might be a more profound brown than when cooked in the oven.

Per serving: Calories: 153; Total fat: 6g; Saturated fat: 3g; Cholesterol: 17mg; Sodium: 211mg; Carbohydrates: 17g; Fiber: 1g; Protein: 7g

SOFT PRETZEL BITES WITH HONEY-MUSTARD DIPPING

SAUCE

FAMILY FAVORITE
VEGETARIAN

Makes 32 pretzel chomps/Prep Time: 20 minutes/Fry Time: 10 minutes

If you love the goliath pretzels or pretzel tears into you can find at the shopping center, you will not have the option to get enough of these nibbles. They are a group top choice at rear end gatherings and patio grills. Change up the flavors by adjusting the plunge or adding a fixing. Sprinkle them with cheddar and garlic or cinnamon-sugar, or plunge them into smooth caramel.

FOR THE PRETZELS

Oil, for spraying
½ cup baking soda
1 (16-ounce) can refrigerated homestyle bread rolls 4 tablespoons unsalted margarine, melted
½ teaspoon granulated garlic
1 tablespoon coarse salt

FOR THE HONEY-MUSTARD DIPPING SAUCE

½ cup mayonnaise
¼ cup yellow mustard
¼ cup honey
Pinch salt

TO MAKE THE PRETZELS

1. Line the air fryer crate with material and shower gently with oil. Line a baking sheet with material paper.
2. Fill a huge stockpot most of the way with water and add the baking pop. Bring to a stew over high heat.
3. Separate the batter and cut every roll into 4 pieces. Fold each piece into a ball.
4. Add half of the batter balls to the stewing water and cook, mixing delicately, for around 2 minutes. Utilizing an opened spoon, move to the pre-arranged baking sheet. Rehash with the leftover dough.
5. Preheat the air fryer to 400°F.
6. In a little bowl, combine as one the dissolved spread and garlic and brush it on the bubbled mixture balls.
7. Place the batter balls in the pre-arranged crate. You might have to

work in groups, contingent upon the size of your air fryer.
8. Cook for 5 minutes, flip, and cook for one more 4 to 5 minutes, or until profound brown.
9. Sprinkle with the coarse salt while still warm.

TO MAKE THE HONEY-MUSTARD DIPPING SAUCE

10. In a little bowl, combine as one the mayonnaise, mustard, honey, and salt.
11. Serve the pretzel chomps with the plunging sauce on the side.

Fry Fact: Don't utilize flaky roll batter, as it will in general self-destruct during the bubbling system. You can top the pretzel chomps with sesame seeds rather than salt, if desired.

Per serving (4 nibbles): Calories: 78; Total fat: 4g; Saturated fat: 1g; Cholesterol: 4mg; Sodium: 1253mg; Carbohydrates: 9g; Fiber: 0g; Protein: 1g

CAN YOU FRY IT?

ROASTED ALMONDS

Line the air fryer basket with parchment and spray lightly with oil. Place the almonds in a single layer in the prepared basket. Cook at 350°F for 5 minutes, or until they smell nutty and are a shade or two darker. If you need to cook them longer, shake the basket after each additional minute. Keep an eye on them, as nuts can burn very easily. Let cool completely before storing in an airtight container.

WAFFLE FRY NACHOS

FAMILY FAVORITE

Serves 4/Prep Time: 5 minutes/Fry Time: 11 minutes

Boost your game-day snacks with this bend on exemplary nachos. Frozen waffle fries make an alternate surface and a good dish that will keep your team feeling full.

Oil, for spraying
1 (20-ounce) bundle frozen waffle fries 1

cup destroyed cheddar cheese
2 tablespoons bacon bits
1 tablespoon canned diced green chiles
1 tablespoon cut olives
¼ cup salsa of choice
1 tablespoon sharp cream

1. Line the air fryer bushel with material and shower gently with oil. Place the waffle fries in the pre-arranged bin and splash softly with oil.
2. Cook at 375°F for 8 minutes. Move to an air fryer-safe baking pan.
3. Top with the cheddar, bacon bits, green chiles, and olives. Increment the hotness to 425°F and cook for 2 to 3 minutes, or until the cheddar is melted.
4. Top with the salsa and acrid cream before serving.

Change It Up: If you need tortilla chips rather than fries, load the crate with similar fixings and cook for 20 minutes at 370°F.

Per serving: Calories: 260; Total fat: 17g; Saturated fat: 6g; Cholesterol: 17mg; Sodium: 532mg; Carbohydrates: 22g; Fiber: 3g; Protein: 6g

BACON-WRAPPED SAUSAGES

FAMILY FAVORITE

Makes 35 hotdogs/Prep Time: 15 minutes/Fry Time: 12 minutes

This happy party tidbit unites sweet and zesty in one radiant nibble. Not a devotee of sweet pork? Utilize zesty grill sauce instead.

Oil, for spraying
1 (12-ounce) bundle thick-cut bacon 1
(12-ounce) bundle mixed drink hotdogs
2 teaspoons stew powder
2 tablespoons maple syrup
2 tablespoons stuffed light earthy colored sugar

1. Line the air fryer bin with material and splash softly with oil. (Try not to skirt the progression of coating the container; the material will get drippings. Assuming your air fryer has an external plate, you can likewise fix it with foil.)
2. Cut each segment of bacon longwise into thirds and fold a piece over

every wiener, getting with a toothpick.
3. Place the enveloped frankfurters by the pre-arranged bin in a solitary layer and sprinkle with the bean stew powder. You might have to work in clumps, contingent upon the size of your air fryer. Brush the frankfurters with the maple syrup and sprinkle with the brown sugar.
4. Cook at 340°F for 6 minutes, flip, and cook for an additional 6 minutes, or until the bacon is crisp.
5. Remove the toothpicks and serve immediately.

Fry Fact: It is more straightforward to wrap the wieners when you're working with cold bacon. This formula additionally works incredible assuming you accomplish the prep work early, cover the hotdogs with saran wrap, and refrigerate until you are prepared to cook. Do a test group of 1 or 2 wieners so you know the ideal measure of time to cook the remainder of them.

Per serving (5 frankfurters): Calories: 278; Total fat: 21g; Saturated fat: 7g; Cholesterol: 53mg; Sodium: 881mg; Carbohydrates: 8g; Fiber: 0g; Protein: 14g

THAI-INSPIRED SWEET CHILI CAULIFLOWER BITES

VEGETARIAN

Serves 6/Prep Time: 15 minutes/Fry Time: 15 minutes

Fried cauliflower has turned into a most loved option in contrast to chicken wings. These chomps aren't battered, yet they actually taste astonishing because of a blazing sauce.

Oil, for spraying
1 medium head cauliflower, cut into florets
2 tablespoons olive oil
2 teaspoons granulated garlic
¼ teaspoon smoked paprika
½ to ¾ cup sweet stew sauce
¼ teaspoon sesame seeds

1. Preheat the air fryer to 400°F. Line the air fryer bushel with material and splash delicately with oil.
2. In a huge bowl, throw the cauliflower with the olive oil until completely covered. Sprinkle with the garlic and paprika and throw

again until coated.

3. Place the cauliflower in the pre-arranged bushel, taking consideration not to cover the pieces. You might have to work in clusters, contingent upon the size of your air fryer.
4. Cook for 15 minutes, flipping at regular intervals, or until seared and crispy.
5. Transfer to a huge bowl and throw with the sweet bean stew sauce and sesame seeds before serving.

Change It Up: Instead of the sweet bean stew sauce, add 1 cup bread scraps and ½ cup ground Parmesan cheddar to the flavors prior to cooking and present with farm dressing. Or then again throw with your beloved grill, bison, or teriyaki sauce.

Per serving: Calories: 86; Total fat: 5g; Saturated fat: 1g; Cholesterol: 0mg; Sodium: 242mg; Carbohydrates: 9g; Fiber: 3g; Protein: 2g

FRIED RAVIOLI

SUPER-FAST

Serves 8/Prep Time: 10 minutes/Fry Time: 5 minutes

The initially seared ravioli emerged from a prevalently Italian St. Louis area during the 1940s, when a bar proprietor dropped a ravioli in oil. Clearly he would rather avoid the sound of "singed ravioli" and alluded to it as toasted all things considered. These firm ravioli pair flawlessly with marinara or garlic-margarine sauce.

Oil, for splashing
2 huge eggs
1 cup panko bread crumbs
¼ cup ground Parmesan cheddar 1 teaspoon onion powder
1 teaspoon granulated garlic
½ teaspoon dry Italian dressing mix
½ teaspoon salt
1 (20-ounce) bundle refrigerated cheddar ravioli

1. Preheat the air fryer to 400°F. Line the air fryer bushel with material and shower softly with oil.
2. In a medium bowl, whisk the eggs and set aside.

3. In another medium bowl, combine as one the bread scraps, Parmesan cheddar, onion powder, garlic, Italian dressing blend, and salt.
4. Add the ravioli to the eggs and throw tenderly to coat.
5. Transfer the ravioli to the bread morsel combination and throw until uniformly coated.
6. Place the ravioli in a solitary layer in the pre-arranged bin. You might have to work in clumps, contingent upon the size of your air fryer. Shower daintily with oil.
7. Cook for 3 to 5 minutes, or until hot and crispy.

Fry Fact: Don't overcook the ravioli or the cheddar will vanish. Diminish or expand the cooking time in view of the size of the ravioli you are using.

Per serving: Calories: 181; Total fat: 7g; Saturated fat: 3g; Cholesterol: 107mg; Sodium: 633mg; Carbohydrates: 20g; Fiber: 1g; Protein: 8g

CHAPTER 4
VEGETABLES AND SIDES

Butter and Garlic Fried Cabbage
Glazed Sweet Potato Bites
Garlic-Parmesan Crispy Baby
Potatoes Buffalo Cauliflower
Bacon Potatoes and Green Beans
Green Bean Fries   Parmesan
Mushrooms Zesty Fried Asparagus
Broccoli-Cheddar Twice-Baked Potatoes
Asian-Inspired Roasted Broccoli Honey
Butter Roasted Carrots
Mexican-Style Street Corn Crispy
Fried Okra   Crispy
Butternut Squash Ranch Kale
Chips   Everything Bagel
Brussels Sprouts Spicy Roasted
Edamame   Fried Green
Tomatoes   Cheesy Zucchini
Chips   Buffalo Chicken
Zucchini Boats

BUFFALO CAULIFLOWER

BUTTER AND GARLIC FRIED

CABBAGE

GLUTEN-FREE
SUPER-FAST
VEGETARIAN

Serves 2/Prep Time: 5 minutes/Fry Time: 9 minutes

Cabbage tastes incredible with only a couple of essential flavors. Air singing it with only a bit of oil and some garlic, salt, and dark pepper creates this light and fresh dish. On the off chance that you're a meat-eater, add ¼ cup bacon bits for a fly of smoky flavor.

Oil, for spraying
½ head cabbage, cut into reduced down
pieces 2 tablespoons unsalted
margarine, melted
1 teaspoon granulated garlic
½ teaspoon coarse ocean salt
¼ teaspoon newly ground dark pepper

1. Line the air fryer bin with material and shower delicately with oil.
2. In an enormous bowl, combine as one the cabbage, spread, garlic, salt, and dark pepper until equally coated.
3. Transfer the cabbage to the pre-arranged bushel and splash gently with oil.
4. Cook at 375°F for 5 minutes, throw, and cook for one more 3 to 4 minutes, or until daintily crispy.

Pair It With: This side dish is great when paired with Honey-Balsamic Salmon, Garlic Butter Steak Bites, or Classic Whole Chicken.

Per serving: Calories: 171; Total fat: 13g; Saturated fat: 8g; Cholesterol: 31mg; Sodium: 423mg; Carbohydrates: 14g; Fiber: 6g; Protein: 3g

GLAZED SWEET POTATO BITES

FAMILY FAVORITE
GLUTEN-FREE
VEGETARIAN

Serves 4/Prep Time: 10 minutes/Fry Time: 25 minutes

Sweet potatoes are an incredible wellspring of fiber and loaded with iron, calcium, selenium, and nutrients B and C. This formula improves them up with a cinnamon-honey glaze.

Oil, for spraying
3 medium yams, stripped and cut into 1-inch pieces 2
tablespoons honey
1 tablespoon olive oil
2 teaspoons ground cinnamon

1. Line the air fryer container with material and shower daintily with oil.
2. In an enormous bowl, throw together the yams, honey, olive oil, and cinnamon until uniformly coated.
3. Place the potatoes in the arranged basket.
4. Cook at 400°F for 20 to 25 minutes, or until fresh and effectively punctured with a fork.

Change It Up: Want your yams considerably better? Add 2 tablespoons stuffed light earthy colored sugar. You can likewise utilize maple syrup rather than honey, if desired.

Per serving: Calories: 149; Total fat: 3g; Saturated fat: 0g; Cholesterol: 0mg; Sodium: 54mg; Carbohydrates: 29g; Fiber: 4g; Protein: 2g

GARLIC-PARMESAN CRISPY BABY POTATOES

GLUTEN-FREE
VEGETARIAN

Serves 4/Prep Time: 10 minutes/Fry Time: 15 minutes

Baby potatoes are stuffed brimming with cancer prevention agents like L-ascorbic acid and minerals like iron. When cooked in the air fryer, they are delicate inside with a delightful firm external skin, making them an ideal side for any dish.

Oil, for spraying
1 pound child potatoes
½ cup ground Parmesan cheddar,
separated 3 tablespoons olive oil

2 teaspoons granulated garlic
½ teaspoon onion powder
½ teaspoon salt
¼ teaspoon newly ground dark pepper
¼ teaspoon paprika
2 tablespoons cleaved new parsley, for garnish

1. Line the air fryer crate with material and splash daintily with oil.
2. Rinse the potatoes, wipe off with paper towels, and spot in a huge bowl.
3. In a little bowl, combine as one ¼ cup of Parmesan cheddar, the olive oil, garlic, onion powder, salt, dark pepper, and paprika. Pour the combination over the potatoes and throw to coat.
4. Transfer the potatoes to the pre-arranged bushel and spread them out in an even layer, taking consideration to hold them back from contacting. You might have to work in clumps, contingent upon the size of your air fryer.
5. Cook at 400°F for 15 minutes, blending following 7 to 8 minutes, or until effectively penetrated with a fork. Keep on cooking for one more 1 to 2 minutes, if needed.
6. Sprinkle with the parsley and the excess Parmesan cheddar and serve.

Pair It With: These potatoes go well with Lemon Pepper Shrimp, Herb Butter Turkey Breast, and Herbed Lamb Steaks.

Per serving: Calories: 234; Total fat: 14g; Saturated fat: 3g; Cholesterol: 11mg; Sodium: 525mg; Carbohydrates: 22g; Fiber: 3g; Protein: 6g

BUFFALO CAULIFLOWER

VEGETARIAN

Serves 4/Prep Time: 10 minutes/Fry Time: 30 minutes

The ascent of plant-based eating regimens has made bison cauliflower very famous. The marginally nutty kind of the cauliflower matches impeccably with the searing sauce.
Serve as a hors d'oeuvre with celery sticks and blue cheddar dressing or as a side with your beloved primary dishes.

Oil, for spraying
1 head cauliflower, cut into florets

2 tablespoons unsalted margarine,
softened 1 tablespoon olive oil
½ cup bison sauce
½ cup almond flour or universally
handy flour 3 tablespoons dried parsley
1 tablespoon granulated garlic
1 teaspoon prepared salt

1. Line the air fryer bushel with material and shower daintily with oil.
2. Place the cauliflower, dissolved spread, olive oil, and hot sauce in a zip-top plastic pack, seal, and throw until equally coated.
3. In a medium bowl, combine as one the almond flour, parsley, garlic, and prepared salt.
4. Add the cauliflower to the flour blend and throw tenderly to coat.
5. Place half of the cauliflower in the arranged basket.
6. Cook at 350°F for 15 minutes, shaking and mixing delicately following 7 or 8 minutes, or until somewhat carmelized however not soft. Rehash with the leftover cauliflower. Serve hot.

Fry Fact: Take care not to pack the air fryer or you will have saturated cauliflower. To warm, cook in the air fryer at 375°F for 4 to 5 minutes, or until hot.

Per serving: Calories: 182; Total fat: 10g; Saturated fat: 4g; Cholesterol: 15mg; Sodium: 856mg; Carbohydrates: 20g; Fiber: 4g; Protein: 5g

BACON POTATOES AND GREEN BEANS

FAMILY FAVORITE

Serves 4/Prep Time: 10 minutes/Fry Time: 25 minutes

Who doesn't adore a tad of bacon to invigorate veggies? This basic, flexible side dish, famous in the South, is generally cooked low and slow. This variant makes it happen in a negligible part of the time without forfeiting any of the flavor.

Oil, for spraying
2 pounds medium chestnut potatoes, quartered
¾ cup bacon bits

10 ounces new green beans
1 teaspoon salt
½ teaspoon newly ground dark pepper

1. Line the air fryer container with material and splash gently with oil.
2. Place the potatoes in the pre-arranged crate. Top with the bacon pieces and green beans. Sprinkle with the salt and dark pepper and shower generously with oil.
3. Cook at 355°F for 25 minutes, mixing following 12 minutes and splashing with oil, until the potatoes are handily punctured with a fork.

Pair It With: Serve with Fried Tilapia, Honey-Glazed Chicken Thighs, or Honey-Garlic Pork Chops.

Per serving: Calories: 258; Total fat: 9g; Saturated fat: 3g; Cholesterol: 23mg; Sodium: 980mg; Carbohydrates: 32g; Fiber: 4g; Protein: 12g

GREEN BEAN FRIES

SUPER-FAST
VEGETARIAN

Serves 6/Prep Time: 5 minutes/Fry Time: 5 minutes

These green bean fries are such a ton more grounded than French fries or potato chips, and they are just as fulfilling on account of their crunchy panko coating.

Oil, for spraying
1 pound new green beans, trimmed
½ cup universally
handy flour 2 huge eggs
1 cup panko bread crumbs
½ cup Parmesan cheddar, in addition to additional for
serving (discretionary) 1 tablespoon granulated garlic

1. Line the air fryer crate with material and splash daintily with oil.
2. If any of the green beans are too long to even consider fitting effectively in the air fryer, cut them in half.
3. Place the green beans and flour in a zip-top plastic pack, seal, and shake well until uniformly coated.

4. In a medium bowl, whisk the eggs.
5. In another medium bowl, combine as one the bread morsels, Parmesan cheddar, and garlic.
6. Working in little groups, plunge the green beans in the eggs, dig in the panko blend until equally covered, and move to the pre-arranged container. You might have to work in groups, contingent upon the size of your air fryer.
7. Cook at 390°F for 5 minutes, or until brilliant brown.
8. Sprinkle with extra Parmesan cheddar, if desired.

Faster Frying: To make these green beans quicker and surprisingly better, skirt the flour. It assists the egg with adhering to the green beans, however they will in any case taste incredible without it.

Per serving: Calories: 158; Total fat: 5g; Saturated fat: 2g; Cholesterol: 69mg; Sodium: 245mg; Carbohydrates: 21g; Fiber: 3g; Protein: 8g

PARMESAN MUSHROOMS

VEGETARIAN

Serves 4/Prep Time: 5 minutes/Fry Time: 15 minutes

If you need to explore different avenues regarding your air fryer, mushrooms are the ideal fixing. The air fryer holds them back from getting soaked or drying out. You can switch around the profile by adding crab, hotdog, spinach, bacon, or shrimp. This formula amps up the umami flavor with Parmesan cheddar and onion soup mix.

Oil, for spraying
1 pound cremini mushrooms, stems managed
2 tablespoons olive oil
2 teaspoons granulated garlic
1 teaspoon dried onion soup mix
½ teaspoon salt
¼ teaspoon newly ground dark pepper
⅓ cup ground Parmesan cheddar, divided

1. Line the air fryer bin with material and splash delicately with oil.
2. In a huge bowl, throw the mushrooms with the olive oil, garlic, onion soup blend, salt, and dark pepper until equally coated.
3. Place the mushrooms in the arranged basket.

4. Cook at 370°F for 13 minutes.
5. Sprinkle half of the cheddar over the mushrooms and cook for another 2 minutes.
6. Transfer the mushrooms to a serving bowl, add the leftover Parmesan cheddar, and throw until equitably covered. Serve immediately.

Pair It With: These mushrooms are great paired with Cornish Game Hens or Herb Butter Turkey Breast.

Per serving: Calories: 121; Total fat: 9g; Saturated fat: 2g; Cholesterol: 7mg; Sodium: 451mg; Carbohydrates: 7g; Fiber: 1g; Protein: 5g

ZESTY FRIED ASPARAGUS

GLUTEN-FREE
SUPER-FAST
VEGETARIAN

Serves 4/Prep Time: 3 minutes/Fry Time: 10 minutes

Roasted asparagus is an incredible wellspring of fiber, folate, and nutrients A, C, and K, and it couldn't be more straightforward to make-you simply need a touch of olive oil and some flavoring. Stew powder gives this form a little bite.

Oil, for spraying
10 to 12 lances asparagus, managed
2 tablespoons olive oil
1 tablespoon granulated garlic
1 teaspoon bean stew powder
½ teaspoon ground cumin
¼ teaspoon salt

1. Line the air fryer bin with material and splash delicately with oil.
2. If the asparagus are too long to even think about fitting effectively in the air fryer, cut them in half.
3. Place the asparagus, olive oil, garlic, bean stew powder, cumin, and salt in a zip-top plastic pack, seal, and throw until equally coated.
4. Place the asparagus in the arranged basket.
5. Cook at 390°F for 5 minutes, flip, and cook for an additional 5 minutes, or until radiant green and firm however tender.

Fry Fact: To set up the asparagus, flush well and remove 1 to 2 crawls of the woody ends.

Per serving: Calories: 74; Total fat: 7g; Saturated fat: 1g; Cholesterol: 0mg; Sodium: 166mg; Carbohydrates: 3g; Fiber: 1g; Protein: 1g

BROCCOLI-CHEDDAR TWICE-BAKED POTATOES

GLUTEN-FREE
VEGETARIAN

Serves 4/Prep Time: 10 minutes/Fry Time: 46 minutes

For this powerful heated potato, you eliminate the tissue and blend it in with broccoli, acrid cream, and cheddar prior to returning it to the potato skin and baking it again.

Oil, for spraying
2 medium reddish brown potatoes 1 tablespoon olive oil
¼ cup broccoli florets
1 tablespoon sharp cream
1 teaspoon granulated garlic
1 teaspoon onion powder
½ cup destroyed cheddar cheese

1. Line the air fryer bin with material and shower gently with oil.
2. Rinse the potatoes and wipe off with paper towels. Rub the outside of the potatoes with the olive oil and spot them in the arranged basket.
3. Cook at 400°F for 40 minutes, or until effectively punctured with a fork. Let cool adequately to deal with, then, at that point, cut the potatoes down the middle lengthwise.
4. Meanwhile, place the broccoli in a microwave-safe bowl, cover with water, and microwave on high for 5 to 8 minutes. Channel and set aside.
5. Scoop out a large portion of the potato tissue and move to a medium bowl.
6. Add the sharp cream, garlic, and onion powder and mix until the potatoes are mashed.
7. Spoon the potato blend once more into the emptied potato skins, mounding it to fit, if fundamental. Top with the broccoli and cheddar. Return the potatoes to the bushel. You might have to work in bunches, depending on
the size of your air fryer.

8. Cook at 400°F for 3 to 6 minutes, or until the cheddar has dissolved. Serve immediately.

Fry Fact: Cook time and temperature will be a similar whether you cook one potato or a few, as long as they fit in the air fryer without crowding.

Per serving: Calories: 244; Total fat: 9g; Saturated fat: 4g; Cholesterol: 16mg; Sodium: 104mg; Carbohydrates: 35g; Fiber: 3g; Protein: 7g

ASIAN-INSPIRED ROASTED BROCCOLI

VEGETARIAN

Serves 4/Prep Time: 10 minutes/Fry Time: 15 minutes

Forget about exhausting steamed broccoli. This adaptation is covered with honey, garlic, and a pleasant kick of sriracha. The air fryer cooks the broccoli uniformly, so every piece is pretty much as firm as the next.

FOR THE BROCCOLI

Oil, for spraying
1 pound broccoli florets
2 teaspoons nut oil
1 tablespoon minced garlic
½ teaspoon salt

FOR THE SAUCE

2 tablespoons soy sauce
2 teaspoons honey
2 teaspoons sriracha
1 teaspoon rice vinegar

TO MAKE THE BROCCOLI

1. Line the air fryer bin with material and shower delicately with oil.
2. In an enormous bowl, throw together the broccoli, nut oil, garlic, and salt until equitably coated.
3. Spread out the broccoli in an even layer in the arranged basket.
4. Cook at 400°F for 15 minutes, blending midway through.

TO MAKE THE SAUCE

5. Meanwhile, in a little microwave-safe bowl, join the soy sauce, honey, sriracha, and rice vinegar and microwave on high for around 15

    seconds. Mix to combine.
6. Transfer the broccoli to a serving bowl and add the sauce. Tenderly throw until equitably covered and serve immediately.

Pair It With: This side dish adds gorgeous color to Teriyaki Salmon or Sesame Chicken.

Per serving: Calories: 77; Total fat: 3g; Saturated fat: 0g; Cholesterol: 0mg; Sodium: 768mg; Carbohydrates: 12g; Fiber: 3g; Protein: 4g

HONEY BUTTER ROASTED CARROTS

GLUTEN-FREE
FAMILY FAVORITE
VEGETARIAN

Serves 4/Prep Time: 5 minutes/Fry Time: 12 minutes

The air fryer plans simmered carrots in a snap, regardless of whether for a Thanksgiving feast or a normal Sunday supper. Honey, margarine, and dill make them considerably more irresistible.

Oil, for spraying
3 cups child carrots
3 tablespoons olive oil
1 tablespoon unsalted spread,
liquefied 1 tablespoon honey
½ teaspoon salt
¼ teaspoon newly ground dark pepper
⅛ teaspoon dried dill, for garnish

1. Line the air fryer bushel with material and shower delicately with oil.
2. In a medium bowl, throw together the carrots, olive oil, margarine, honey, salt, and dark pepper until uniformly coated.
3. Place the carrots in the arranged basket.
4. Cook at 390°F for 12 minutes, until cooked through.
5. Transfer to a serving bowl, sprinkle with the dill, and serve.

Change It Up: Keep it basic simply by throwing the carrots in olive oil and salt. Or then again make the dish considerably more delightful by adding 1 teaspoon balsamic vinegar or a few portions of earthy colored sugar. In the event that you can't find child carrots, strip and cleave 1 or 2 huge carrots.

Per serving: Calories: 169; Total fat: 13g; Saturated fat: 3g; Cholesterol: 8mg; Sodium: 377mg; Carbohydrates: 13g; Fiber: 3g; Protein: 1g

MEXICAN-STYLE STREET CORN

FAMILY FAVORITE
GLUTEN-FREE
VEGETARIAN

Serves 4/Prep Time: 10 minutes/Fry Time: 15 minutes

Traditionally served on a stick, this Mexican road nibble, now and again called elote, covers an ear of corn with scrumptious feta cheddar, bean stew powder, and stone house preparing, which is a mix of salt, dark pepper, and garlic.

Oil, for spraying
4 ears corn, shucked
¼ cup disintegrated feta cheese
¼ teaspoon bean stew powder
¼ teaspoon salt
¼ teaspoon granulated garlic
⅛ teaspoon newly ground dark pepper
¼ cup slashed new cilantro 1
tablespoon lime juice

1. Line the air fryer bin with material and splash daintily with oil.
2. Place the corn in the arranged basket.
3. Cook at 390°F for 10 minutes.
4. Sprinkle the corn with the feta cheddar and keep on cooking for an additional 5 minutes.
5. Move to a serving plate and sprinkle with the stew powder, salt, garlic, dark pepper, and cilantro. Not long prior to serving, shower with the lime juice.

Faster Frying: To make this formula considerably quicker, you can make your own flavoring blend early and have it close by to use in plans like this. Combine as one ¼ cup genuine salt, 2 tablespoons newly ground dark pepper, and 2 teaspoons granulated garlic. Use about ½ teaspoon in this formula instead of the salt, dark pepper, and granulated garlic. Store in an impermeable container.

Per serving: Calories: 149; Total fat: 3g; Saturated fat: 2g; Cholesterol: 8mg; Sodium: 243mg; Carbohydrates: 30g; Fiber: 4g; Protein: 6g

CRISPY FRIED OKRA

VEGETARIAN

Serves 6/Prep Time: 5 minutes/Fry Time: 12 minutes

Okra is a blooming vegetable in a similar family as hibiscus. At the point when the cases are youthful, they are frequently utilized for soups, stews, or canning. But they can also be coated in a cornmeal-flour mixture and fried into a crunchy snack or side dish.

Oil, for splashing
1 enormous egg
¼ cup buttermilk
½ cup universally handy flour
½ cup yellow cornmeal
½ teaspoon salt
¼ teaspoon newly ground dark pepper 1
pound okra, managed and cut into slices

1. Preheat the air fryer to 400°F. Line the air fryer crate with material and shower daintily with oil.
2. In a shallow bowl, whisk together the egg and buttermilk.
3. In a medium bowl, combine as one the flour, cornmeal, salt, and dark pepper.
4. Toss the okra cuts in the egg blend, then, at that point, dig in the flour combination until equally covered, shaking off any excess.
5. Place the okra in the pre-arranged container. For most extreme crunch, splash daintily with oil. You might have to work in groups, contingent upon the size of your air fryer.
6. Cook for 10 to 12 minutes, shaking and splashing with more oil following 4 minutes and following 7 minutes, until brilliant brown.
7. Sprinkle with extra salt, whenever wanted, and serve.

Fry Fact: When looking for okra, search for a uniformly green tone and cases that are 2 to 4 inches long. Stay away from any that look wilted or are delicate when crushed. Okra should snap, instead of twisting. You don't need to eliminate the fluff on the okra, however assuming you need to, run them submerged and rub gently with a wet paper towel. To keep the okra from getting disgusting during cooking, absorb entire okra ½ cup white vinegar for around 30 minutes prior to cooking. Wash well and dry completely prior to cutting into slices.

Per serving: Calories: 124; Total fat: 2g; Saturated fat: 1g; Cholesterol: 31mg; Sodium: 231mg; Carbohydrates: 21g; Fiber: 4g; Protein: 5g

CRISPY BUTTERNUT SQUASH

VEGETARIAN

Serves 4/Prep Time: 15 minutes/Fry Time: 17 minutes

Butternut squash is more flexible than you may might suspect. It's regularly added to soups and stews to provide them with a sound portion of key nutrients and supplements, yet it's comparable all alone. This air-fried version is delicious served with a white bean dip, utilized in servings of mixed greens, or blended in with Everything Bagel Brussels Sprouts.

Oil, for spraying
1 butternut squash, cut into 1-inch solid shapes 1 tablespoon olive oil
1 tablespoon maple syrup
1 teaspoon ground cinnamon

1. Line the air fryer bin with material and splash delicately with oil.
2. In an enormous bowl, throw the squash with the olive oil, maple syrup, and cinnamon until uniformly coated.
3. Place the squash in the arranged basket.
4. Cook at 400°F for 17 minutes, shaking and mixing following 9 minutes, until tender.

Fry Fact: To set up the squash, utilize a sharp blade to painstakingly cut about ¼ inch off each end. Eliminate the skin with a vegetable peeler. Stand the squash upstanding and cut down the middle start to finish. Scratch out the seeds with a spoon, cut the parts into cuts, and cut the cuts into cubes.

Per serving: Calories: 123; Total fat: 4g; Saturated fat: 1g; Cholesterol: 0mg; Sodium: 8mg; Carbohydrates: 24g; Fiber: 4g; Protein: 2g

RANCH KALE CHIPS

> GLUTEN-FREE
> SUPER-FAST
> VEGETARIAN

Serves 2/Prep Time: 5 minutes/Fry Time: 5 minutes

Kale chips make a delectable, solid option in contrast to potato chips. They're similarly as crunchy, and you can enhance them in incalculable various ways. This formula utilizes farm preparing to make a game day-commendable treat.

Oil, for spraying
4 cups approximately stuffed stemmed and torn kale 2 tablespoons olive oil
2 tablespoons dry farm seasoning
¼ teaspoon salt

1. Line the air fryer bin with material and shower daintily with oil.
2. In a huge bowl, throw the kale, olive oil, farm preparing, and salt until equitably coated.
3. Place the kale in the pre-arranged bushel. You might have to work in groups, contingent upon the size of your air fryer.
4. Cook at 370°F for 4 to 5 minutes, shaking following 2 minutes, until crispy.

Fry Fact: Remove the kale stems since they take significantly longer to cook than the leaves. Store them in a hermetically sealed compartment in the fridge and add them to your next stew.

Per serving: Calories: 135; Total fat: 14g; Saturated fat: 2g; Cholesterol: 0mg; Sodium: 303mg; Carbohydrates: 3g; Fiber: 1g; Protein: 1g

CAN YOU FRY IT?

RADISHES

Line the air fryer basket with parchment and spray lightly with oil. Cut the radishes into slices and spread them out in a single layer in the prepared basket. Spray lightly with oil and sprinkle with salt, freshly ground black pepper, and onion powder. Cook at 370°F for 18 to 20 minutes, shaking and spraying with oil every 5 minutes.

EVERYTHING BAGEL BRUSSELS SPROUTS

VEGETARIAN

Serves 8/Prep Time: 15 minutes/Fry Time: 15 minutes

The kinds of the universally adored bagel beating sesame seeds, garlic, and onion-work out positively for pretty much everything (normally), including Brussels sprouts. Why not join the two for a fun and delectable side dish?

Oil, for spraying
1½ pounds Brussels sprouts, trimmed
¼ cup ground Parmesan cheese
¼ cup finely hacked almonds 2
tablespoons olive oil
2 tablespoons everything bagel seasoning

1. Line the air fryer container with material and splash daintily with oil.
2. Bring an enormous pot of water to a bubble over high hotness. Add the Brussels fledglings and cook until recently mellowed, 8 to 10 minutes. Channel and let cool sufficiently long that you can deal with them.
3. Cut the fledglings down the middle. Place the fledglings, Parmesan cheddar, almonds, olive oil, and preparing in a zip-top plastic pack, seal, and throw until uniformly coated.
4. Place the fledglings in the arranged basket.
5. Cook at 390°F for 12 to 15 minutes, blending following 6 to 8 minutes, or until brilliant on both sides.

Fry Fact: You can purchase all that bagel preparing all things considered stores or make your own by consolidating 1 tablespoon dark sesame seeds, 1 tablespoon standard sesame seeds, 1 teaspoon granulated garlic, 1 teaspoon onion powder, and a touch of salt. Store in an impermeable compartment at room temperature.

Per serving: Calories: 99; Total fat: 6g; Saturated fat: 4g; Cholesterol: 3mg; Sodium: 432mg; Carbohydrates: 9g; Fiber: 4g; Protein: 4g

SPICY ROASTED EDAMAME

SUPER-FAST
VEGETARIAN

Serves 4/Prep Time: 5 minutes/Fry Time: 10 minutes

High in protein and iron, edamame became well known in the United States as a bite usually served at Japanese cafés. Presently individuals serve them with a wide range of cooking. They emerge from the air fryer crunchy and overflowing with flavor.

Oil, for spraying
2 cups shelled edamame
1 tablespoon olive oil
1 teaspoon hot sauce
½ teaspoon granulated garlic
Pinch salt, for serving

1. Line the air fryer crate with material and splash gently with oil.
2. In a medium bowl, throw together the edamame, olive oil, hot sauce, and garlic until uniformly coated.
3. Place the edamame in the arranged basket.
4. Cook at 390°F for 10 minutes, blending following 5 minutes, until crunchy. Assuming that you need the edamame to be even crunchier, cook for an additional 5 minutes. Add salt to taste.

Change It Up: The flavor prospects are for all intents and purposes perpetual. Take a stab at adding sesame seeds, dry farm preparing, dried onion soup blend, ground Parmesan cheddar, minced garlic, or dried cranberries, or mixing the edamame into Taco-Spiced Chickpeas.

Per serving: Calories: 95; Total fat: 6g; Saturated fat: 0g; Cholesterol: 0mg; Sodium: 50mg; Carbohydrates: 5g; Fiber: 3g; Protein: 6g

FRIED GREEN TOMATOES

SUPER-FAST
VEGETARIAN

Serves 4/Prep Time: 5 minutes/Fry Time: 8 minutes

This exemplary Southern dish includes meagerly cut green tomatoes that have been prepared, covered with cornmeal, and singed in bacon fat. In this better take, the tomatoes are covered in panko bread scraps (which means less cornmeal) and air seared with simply a light moistening of oil.

Oil, for spraying
2 green (unripe) tomatoes, cut into slices
½ teaspoon salt
¼ teaspoon newly ground dark pepper
½ cup generally useful
flour 2 huge eggs
½ cup buttermilk
1 cup panko bread pieces 1
cup yellow cornmeal

1. Preheat the air fryer to 400°F. Line the air fryer crate with material and splash delicately with oil.
2. Season the tomato cuts with salt and dark pepper.
3. Place the flour on a shallow plate.
4. In a little bowl, whisk together the eggs and buttermilk.
5. Combine the bread scraps and cornmeal on one more shallow plate.
6. Dredge the tomato cuts in the flour, dunk in the egg blend, and coat with the panko bread morsels on both sides.
7. Place the tomato cuts in the pre-arranged container and shower daintily with oil. You might have to work in bunches, contingent upon the size of your air fryer.
8. Cook for 5 minutes, flip, and cook for an additional 3 minutes, or until brilliant brown on both sides.

Fry Fact: Serve with the traditionally Southern rebound sauce for plunging. In a bowl, combine as one ½ cup mayonnaise, 1 tablespoon ketchup, 1 teaspoon lemon juice, ½ teaspoon hot sauce, ½ teaspoon paprika, ½ teaspoon granulated garlic, ½ teaspoon dry mustard, and ½ teaspoon salt. Refrigerate until prepared to serve.

Per serving: Calories: 304; Total fat: 7g; Saturated fat: 2g; Cholesterol: 94mg; Sodium: 497mg; Carbohydrates: 50g; Fiber: 5g; Protein: 12g

CHEESY ZUCCHINI CHIPS

GLUTEN-FREE
VEGETARIAN

Serves 2/Prep Time: 10 minutes/Fry Time: 12 minutes

These sound zucchini chips have only two fixings, and it's difficult to express what's really astounding the way in which delectable they are or that they are so natural to make.
Serve them alone or plunge them in farm dressing or marinara sauce.

Oil, for spraying
1 medium zucchini, cut into ¼-inch-thick slices
½ cup ground Parmesan
cheddar Pinch salt (optional)

1. Line the air fryer container with material and shower daintily with oil.
2. Place the zucchini in a solitary layer in the pre-arranged crate. You might have to work in bunches, contingent upon the size of your air fryer.
3. Sprinkle the zucchini with the Parmesan cheddar, covering the highest points of each chip.
4. Cook at 370°F for 10 to 12 minutes, or until the cheddar is dim brilliant brown. The zucchini will fresh as it cools.
5. Sprinkle with the salt (if utilizing) before serving.

Change It Up: For crispier chips, utilize a mandoline to cut the zucchini into ⅛-inch-thick cuts. Take a stab at throwing the cuts with olive oil and a touch of salt; taco preparing, salt, and vinegar; finely hacked almonds and destroyed cheddar; or a little sprinkle of panko bread scraps before air frying.

Per serving: Calories: 122; Total fat: 7g; Saturated fat: 4g; Cholesterol: 22mg; Sodium: 459mg; Carbohydrates: 7g; Fiber: 1g; Protein: 8g

BUFFALO CHICKEN ZUCCHINI BOATS

FAMILY FAVORITE
SUPER-FAST

Serves 4/Prep Time: 5 minutes/Fry Time: 9 minutes

Combine the zesty fieriness of hot sauce with wet rotisserie chicken, cream cheddar, and fresh air-seared zucchini, and you have a generous, ache for commendable dish that functions admirably as a primary course or on the side.

Oil, for spraying
2 medium zucchini, cut down the middle lengthwise
2 cups destroyed rotisserie or extra chicken 3
ounces cream cheddar, softened
¼ cup farm dressing
½ cup destroyed cheddar 2
tablespoons bison sauce
½ cup destroyed mozzarella cheese

1. Preheat the air fryer to 390°F. Line the air fryer container with material and shower delicately with oil.
2. Using a spoon, scratch out the inward tissue of the zucchini, leaving about ¼ inch as far as possible around, to make a boat.
3. Place the boats in the arranged basket.
4. Cook for 3 to 5 minutes, or until simply beginning to blister.
5. In a medium bowl, combine as one the chicken, cream cheddar, farm dressing, cheddar, and bison sauce.
6. Spoon the chicken combination into the boats, isolating equally. Top each with mozzarella cheese.
7. Cook for 4 minutes, or until the cheddar is liquefied and the chicken combination is warmed through.

Change It Up: To ease up this formula, utilize canned fish or salmon rather than chicken.

Per serving: Calories: 360; Total fat: 25g; Saturated fat: 11g; Cholesterol: 105mg; Sodium: 481mg; Carbohydrates: 5g; Fiber: 1g; Protein: 28g

CHAPTER 5
FISH AND SHELLFISH

Tuna Melt
Fried Tilapia
Panko-Crusted Fish Sticks
Lemon Mahi-Mahi Cod
with Creamy Mustard Sauce
Catfish Bites
Honey-Balsamic Salmon
Teriyaki Salmon Cajun
Shrimp Fried Garlic
Shrimp Lemon Pepper
Shrimp Shrimp Kebabs
Thai-Style Shrimp Stir-Fry
Crab Cakes Classic
French Mussels Hot Crab
Dip
10-Minute Garlic-Pesto Scallops
Crispy Fried Calamari

SHRIMP KEBABS

TUNA MELT

SUPER-FAST

Makes 1 sandwich/Prep Time: 3 minutes/Fry Time: 10 minutes

This fantastic exemplary sandwich is so natural to make in the air fryer. Use your extra energy to set up a side salad.

Oil, for spraying
½ (5-ounce) can fish, depleted
1 tablespoon mayonnaise
¼ teaspoon granulated garlic, in addition to
additional for decorate 2 teaspoons unsalted butter
2 cuts sandwich bread 2
cuts cheddar cheese

1. Line the air fryer bin with material and splash delicately with oil.
2. In a medium bowl, combine as one the fish, mayonnaise, and garlic.
3. Spread 1 teaspoon of margarine on each cut of bread and spot one cut spread side down in the arranged basket.
4. Top with a cut of cheddar, the fish blend, one more cut of cheddar, and the other cut of bread, spread side up.
5. Cook at 400°F for 5 minutes, flip, and cook for an additional 5 minutes, until carmelized and crispy.
6. Sprinkle with extra garlic prior to slicing down the middle and serving.

Change It Up: Experiment with various bread types, like entire wheat or sourdough, and flavor the fish combination with finely hacked celery, poppy seeds, hot sauce, squashed potato chips, or pickle relish.

Per serving (1 sandwich): Calories: 480; Total fat: 30g; Saturated fat: 12g; Cholesterol: 75mg; Sodium: 764mg; Carbohydrates: 28g; Fiber: 2g; Protein: 24g

FRIED TILAPIA

FAMILY FAVORITE

Serves 4/Prep Time: 15 minutes/Fry Time: 6 minutes

Tilapia is a gentle freshwater fish that makes a solid weeknight feast. The light panko covering gives it a crunchy outside, while the fryer's even air dissemination keeps the fish totally flaky inside.

Oil, for spraying
1 cup panko bread crumbs
2 tablespoons Old Bay flavoring

2 teaspoons granulated garlic
1 teaspoon onion powder
½ teaspoon salt
¼ teaspoon newly ground dark pepper 1
huge egg
4 tilapia fillets

1. Preheat the air fryer to 400°F. Line the air fryer crate with material and shower daintily with oil.
2. In a shallow bowl, combine as one the bread morsels, Old Bay, garlic, onion powder, salt, and dark pepper.
3. In a little bowl, whisk the egg.
4. Coat the tilapia in the egg, then, at that point, dig in the bread piece blend until totally coated.
5. Place the tilapia in the pre-arranged container. You might have to work in groups, contingent upon the size of your air fryer. Splash daintily with oil.
6. Cook for 4 to 6 minutes, contingent upon the thickness of the filets, until the inner temperature arrives at 145°F. Serve immediately.

Pair It With: Fried tilapia is commonly served with French fries or coleslaw, but it's also wonderful served with Garlic-Parmesan Crispy Baby Potatoes, Bacon Potatoes and Green Beans, or Butter and Garlic Fried Cabbage.

Per serving: Calories: 221; Total fat: 5g; Saturated fat: 2g; Cholesterol: 117mg; Sodium: 1182mg; Carbohydrates: 11g; Fiber: 1g; Protein: 32g

PANKO-CRUSTED FISH STICKS

FAMILY FAVORITE

Serves 4/Prep Time: 10 minutes/Fry Time: 15 minutes

Fish sticks are a child well disposed staple, however this formula is a complex update with Creole flavoring and exemplary tartar sauce.

FOR THE TARTAR SAUCE

2 cups mayonnaise
2 tablespoons dill pickle relish
1 tablespoon dried minced onions

FOR THE FISH STICKS

Oil, for spraying
1 pound tilapia fillets
½ cup universally handy flour
2 cups panko bread crumbs
2 tablespoons Creole flavoring
2 teaspoons granulated garlic
1 teaspoon onion powder
½ teaspoon salt
¼ teaspoon newly ground dark pepper
1 huge egg

TO MAKE THE TARTAR SAUCE

1. In a little bowl, whisk together the mayonnaise, pickle relish, and onions. Cover with saran wrap and refrigerate until prepared to serve. You can make this sauce early; the flavors will heighten as it chills.

TO MAKE THE FISH STICKS

2. Preheat the air fryer to 350°F. Line the air fryer crate with material and shower daintily with oil.
3. Cut the filets into equivalent size sticks and spot them in a compress top plastic bag.
4. Add the flour to the pack, seal, and shake well until uniformly coated.
5. In a shallow bowl, combine as one the bread scraps, Creole flavoring, garlic, onion powder, salt, and dark pepper.
6. In a little bowl, whisk the egg.
7. Dip the fish sticks in the egg, then, at that point, dig in the bread piece combination until totally coated.
8. Place the fish sticks in the pre-arranged bushel. You might have to work in clumps, contingent upon the size of your air fryer. Try not to stuff. Shower daintily with oil.
9. Cook for 12 to 15 minutes, or until sautéed and cooked through. Present with the tartar sauce.

Faster Frying: Need supper instantly? You can cook frozen fish sticks or little breaded filets in your air fryer, as well. Cook at 400°F for 4 minutes, flip, and cook for an additional 4 minutes. Jazz them up by sprinkling with salt, granulated garlic, or Creole, Old Bay, taco, or farm seasoning.

Per presenting (with 2 tablespoons tartar sauce): Calories: 502; Total fat: 26g; Saturated fat: 5g; Cholesterol: 115mg; Sodium: 802mg; Carbohydrates: 35g; Fiber: 2g; Protein: 30g

CAN YOU FRY IT?

LOBSTER TAILS

Line the air fryer basket with parchment and spray lightly with oil. Butterfly the lobster tails by cutting open the top and sliding your finger under the shell to remove the meat. Lay the meat on top of the shell. Place in the prepared basket and brush with melted butter. Cook at 380°F for 4 minutes, brush with more butter, and cook for another 3 to 4 minutes, until opaque and the internal temperature reaches 140°F.

LEMON MAHI-MAHI

GLUTEN-FREE

Serves 2/Prep Time: 5 minutes/Fry Time: 14 minutes

Also known as dolphinfish or dorado, mahi-mahi is generally found in tropical waters, yet you can buy it at most supermarkets. Its firm, lean meat is somewhat sweet and yields huge, sodden pieces. Only a tad piece of lemon and dill is the ideal complement.

Oil, for spraying
2 (6-ounce) mahi-mahi filets
1 tablespoon lemon juice
1 tablespoon olive oil
¼ teaspoon salt
¼ teaspoon newly ground dark pepper 1 tablespoon hacked new dill
2 lemon slices

1. Line the air fryer crate with material and splash delicately with oil.
2. Place the mahi-mahi in the arranged basket.
3. In a little bowl, whisk together the lemon juice and olive oil. Brush the blend equitably over the mahi-mahi.

4. Sprinkle the mahi-mahi with the salt and dark pepper and top with the dill.
5. Cook at 400°F for 12 to 14 minutes, contingent upon the thickness of the filets, until they piece easily.
6. Transfer to plates, top each with a lemon cut, and serve.

Pair It With: Serve with Zesty Fried Asparagus, Crispy Butternut Squash, or Glazed Sweet Potato Bites.

Per serving: Calories: 187; Total fat: 7g; Saturated fat: 1g; Cholesterol: 92mg; Sodium: 553mg; Carbohydrates: 1g; Fiber: 0g; Protein: 28g

COD WITH CREAMY MUSTARD SAUCE

GLUTEN-FREE

Serves 4/Prep Time: 10 minutes/Fry Time: 10 minutes

If you are eating light, cod is an extraordinary decision. It's low in calories and fat, settling on it a characteristic decision for the air fryer. Serve it with a side of new vegetables and utilize any extras in tacos or chowder.

FOR THE FISH

Oil, for showering
1 pound cod fillets
2 tablespoons olive oil
1 tablespoon lemon juice
1 teaspoon salt
½ teaspoon newly ground dark pepper

FOR THE MUSTARD SAUCE

½ cup weighty cream
3 tablespoons Dijon mustard
1 tablespoon unsalted spread
1 teaspoon salt

TO MAKE THE FISH

1. Line the air fryer container with material and splash gently with oil.
2. Rub the cod with the olive oil and lemon juice. Season with the salt and dark pepper.

3. Place the cod in the pre-arranged bushel. You might have to work in bunches, contingent upon the size of your air fryer.
4. Cook at 350°F for 5 minutes. Increment the temperature to 400°F and cook for an additional 5 minutes, until flaky and the inner temperature arrives at 145°F.

TO MAKE THE MUSTARD SAUCE

5. In a little pan, combine as one the weighty cream, mustard, margarine, and salt and bring to a stew over low hotness. Cook for 3 to 4 minutes, or until the sauce starts to thicken.
6. Transfer the cod to a serving plate and shower with the mustard sauce. Serve right away.

Pair It With: Serve with Bacon Potatoes and Green Beans or Everything Bagel Brussels Sprouts.

Per serving: Calories: 274; Total fat: 22g; Saturated fat: 10g; Cholesterol: 102mg; Sodium: 1670mg; Carbohydrates: 2g; Fiber: 1g; Protein: 18g

CATFISH BITES

Serves 4 / Prep Time: 15 minutes / Fry Time: 20 minutes

You haven't truly tasted Southern food until you've enjoyed fried catfish. Try dipping these delicious bites in Cajun sauce or Tartar Sauce (here and serving with a side of Fried Pickle Chips.

Oil, for spraying
1 pound catfish fillets, cut into 2-inch pieces
1 cup buttermilk
½ cup cornmeal
¼ cup all-purpose flour
2 teaspoons Creole seasoning
½ cup yellow mustard

1. Line the air fryer basket with parchment and spray lightly with oil.
2. Place the catfish pieces and buttermilk in a zip-top plastic bag, seal, and refrigerate for about 10 minutes.
3. In a shallow bowl, mix together the cornmeal, flour, and Creole seasoning.
4. Remove the catfish from the bag and pat dry with a paper towel.
5. Spread the mustard on all sides of the catfish, then dip them in

the cornmeal mixture until evenly coated.
6. Place the catfish in the prepared basket. You may need to work in batches, depending on the size of your air fryer. Spray lightly with oil.
7. Cook at 400°F for 10 minutes, flip carefully, spray with oil, and cook for another 10 minutes. Serve immediately.

Faster Frying: Make this recipe even lighter by eliminating the buttermilk and mustard. Simply dredge the catfish pieces in the cornmeal mixture before cooking.

Per serving: Calories: 247; Total fat: 7g; Saturated fat: 2g; Cholesterol: 68mg; Sodium: 510mg; Carbohydrates: 22g; Fiber: 3g; Protein: 24g

HONEY-BALSAMIC SALMON

GLUTEN-FREE
SUPER-FAST

Serves 2 / Prep Time: 5 minutes / Fry Time: 8 minutes

Who knew it would be so easy to create juicy, flaky salmon fillets in an air fryer? The honey and balsamic vinegar paired with red pepper flakes give a sweetness with a bit of zest. This recipe is great for weeknight dinners or a special luncheon.

Oil, for spraying
2 (6-ounce) salmon fillets
¼ cup balsamic vinegar
2 tablespoons honey
2 teaspoons red pepper flakes
2 teaspoons olive oil
½ teaspoon salt
¼ teaspoon freshly ground black pepper

1. Line the air fryer basket with parchment and spray lightly with oil.
2. Place the salmon in the prepared basket.
3. In a small bowl, whisk together the balsamic vinegar, honey, red pepper flakes, olive oil, salt, and black pepper. Brush the mixture over the salmon.
4. Cook at 390°F for 7 to 8 minutes, or until the internal temperature reaches 145°F. Serve immediately.

Change It Up: Mix together 1½ tablespoons melted butter, 1 tablespoon garlic, 1 tablespoon lemon juice, 2 teaspoons packed light brown sugar, 2 teaspoons chopped fresh parsley, and ½ teaspoon dried Italian seasoning and brush the sauce over the salmon before cooking.

Per serving: Calories: 373; Total fat: 15g; Saturated fat: 2g; Cholesterol: 94mg; Sodium: 664mg; Carbohydrates: 23g; Fiber: 0g; Protein: 34g

TERIYAKI SALMON

FAMILY FAVORITE

Serves 4 / Prep Time: 6 minutes, plus 30 minutes to marinate / Fry Time: 12 minutes

The mild flavor of salmon pairs well with a variety of marinades, including the sweet ginger-powered flavor of teriyaki sauce. The air fryer cooks the fish quickly, creating the perfect outside crust while keeping the inside moist and juicy.

4 (6-ounce) salmon fillets
½ cup soy sauce
¼ cup packed light brown sugar
2 teaspoons rice vinegar
1 teaspoon minced garlic
¼ teaspoon ground ginger
2 teaspoons olive oil
½ teaspoon salt
¼ teaspoon freshly ground black pepper
Oil, for spraying

1. Place the salmon in a small pan, skin-side up.
2. In a small bowl, whisk together the soy sauce, brown sugar, rice vinegar, garlic, ginger, olive oil, salt, and black pepper.
3. Pour the mixture over the salmon and marinate for about 30 minutes.
4. Line the air fryer basket with parchment and spray lightly with oil. Place the salmon in the prepared basket, skin-side down. You may need to work in batches, depending on the size of your air fryer.
5. Cook at 400°F for 6 minutes, brush the salmon with more marinade, and cook for another 6 minutes, or until the internal temperature reaches 145°F. Serve immediately.

Pair It With: Garlic-Parmesan Crispy Baby Potatoes or Honey Butter Roasted Carrots make a lovely accompaniment for this dish.

Per serving: Calories: 276; Total fat: 13g; Saturated fat: 2g; Cholesterol: 94mg; Sodium: 806mg; Carbohydrates: 3g; Fiber: 0g; Protein: 34g

CAJUN SHRIMP

FAMILY FAVORITE

Serves 4 / Prep Time: 15 minutes / Fry Time: 9 minutes

Louisiana is known for distinct, bold, and exciting Cajun flavors. This spicy shrimp, mixed with kielbasa and vegetables, is sure to transport you to the bayou.

Oil, for spraying
1 pound jumbo raw shrimp, peeled and deveined
1 tablespoon Cajun seasoning
6 ounces cooked kielbasa, cut into thick slices
½ medium zucchini, cut into ¼-inch-thick slices
½ medium yellow squash, cut into ¼-inch-thick slices
1 green bell pepper, seeded and cut into 1-inch pieces
2 tablespoons olive oil
½ teaspoon salt

1. Preheat the air fryer to 400°F. Line the air fryer basket with parchment and spray lightly with oil.
2. In a large bowl, toss together the shrimp and Cajun seasoning. Add the kielbasa, zucchini, squash, bell pepper, olive oil, and salt and mix well.
3. Transfer the mixture to the prepared basket, taking care not to overcrowd. You may need to work in batches, depending on the size of your air fryer.
4. Cook for 9 minutes, shaking and stirring every 3 minutes. Serve immediately.

Change It Up: Replace the Cajun flavors with a light coating of olive oil, salt, and black pepper. Or swap the zucchini for green beans, corn, or other favorite vegetables.

Per serving: Calories: 251; Total fat: 16g; Saturated fat: 4g; Cholesterol: 173mg; Sodium: 1148mg; Carbohydrates: 6g; Fiber: 1g; Protein: 22g

FRIED GARLIC SHRIMP

Serves 3 / Prep Time: 15 minutes / Fry Time: 10 minutes

Deep-fried breaded shrimp has been popular in the United States since packaged frozen shrimp came on the market after World War II. Making this

dish in the air fryer saves about 20 minutes, as well as a ton of calories and fat. Garlic butter sauce gives the dish even more flavor.

FOR THE SHRIMP

Oil, for spraying
1 pound medium raw shrimp, peeled and deveined 6
tablespoons unsalted butter, melted
1 cup panko bread crumbs
2 tablespoons granulated garlic 1
teaspoon salt
½ teaspoon freshly ground black pepper

FOR THE GARLIC BUTTER SAUCE

½ cup unsalted butter
2 teaspoons granulated garlic
¾ teaspoon salt (omit if using salted butter)

TO MAKE THE SHRIMP

1. Preheat the air fryer to 400°F. Line the air fryer basket with parchment and spray lightly with oil.
2. Place the shrimp and melted butter in a zip-top plastic bag, seal, and shake well, until evenly coated.
3. In a medium bowl, mix together the bread crumbs, garlic, salt, and black pepper.
4. Add the shrimp to the panko mixture and toss until evenly coated. Shake off any excess coating.
5. Place the shrimp in the prepared basket and spray lightly with oil.
6. Cook for 8 to 10 minutes, flipping and spraying with oil after 4 to 5 minutes, until golden brown and crispy.

TO MAKE THE GARLIC BUTTER SAUCE

7. In a microwave-safe bowl, combine the butter, garlic, and salt and microwave on 50% power for 30 to 60 seconds, stirring every 15 seconds, until completely melted.
8. Serve the shrimp immediately with the garlic butter sauce on the side for dipping.

Fry Fact: If you need to quickly thaw frozen shrimp, place them in a bowl of cool water.

Per serving: Calories: 352; Total fat: 25g; Saturated fat: 15g; Cholesterol: 252mg; Sodium: 1218mg; Carbohydrates: 9g; Fiber: 1g; Protein: 22g

LEMON PEPPER SHRIMP

GLUTEN-FREE

Serves 2 / Prep Time: 15 minutes / Fry Time: 8 minutes

A healthier, low-carb alternative to breaded popcorn shrimp, this recipe is bursting with lemon pepper flavor and couldn't be easier to prepare. It makes a perfect appetizer, or pair it with rice for a full meal.

Oil, for spraying
12 ounces medium raw shrimp, peeled and deveined
3 tablespoons lemon juice
1 tablespoon olive oil
1 teaspoon lemon pepper
¼ teaspoon paprika
¼ teaspoon granulated garlic

1. Preheat the air fryer to 400°F. Line the air fryer basket with parchment and spray lightly with oil.
2. In a medium bowl, toss together the shrimp, lemon juice, olive oil, lemon pepper, paprika, and garlic until evenly coated.
3. Place the shrimp in the prepared basket.
4. Cook for 6 to 8 minutes, or until pink and firm. Serve immediately.

Fry Fact: You can remove the tails, if desired, or keep them on. Be careful not to overcook, which can happen quickly. Cook until just pink and no longer translucent.

Per serving: Calories: 187; Total fat: 9g; Saturated fat: 1g; Cholesterol: 214mg; Sodium: 853mg; Carbohydrates: 3g; Fiber: 0g; Protein: 23g

SHRIMP KEBABS

FAMILY FAVORITE

Serves 4 / Prep Time: 15 minutes / Fry Time: 6 minutes

Thanks to the air fryer, you can enjoy these kebabs all year, even when it's too cold to fire up the grill. Old Bay seasoning, the perfect seafood spice, makes these a huge hit at any gathering. You'll need 4 metal skewers; make sure they fit in the air fryer.

Oil, for spraying
1 pound medium raw shrimp, peeled and deveined
4 tablespoons unsalted butter, melted
1 tablespoon Old Bay seasoning
1 tablespoon packed light brown sugar
1 teaspoon granulated garlic
1 teaspoon onion powder
½ teaspoon freshly ground black pepper

1. Line the air fryer basket with parchment and spray lightly with oil.
2. Thread the shrimp onto the skewers and place them in the prepared basket.
3. In a small bowl, mix together the butter, Old Bay, brown sugar, garlic, onion powder, and black pepper. Brush the sauce on the shrimp.
4. Cook at 400°F for 5 to 6 minutes, or until pink and firm. Serve immediately.

Change It Up: Shrimp are incredibly versatile. Try adding chunks of onion, green bell pepper, or zucchini to the skewer. You can also switch up the flavor with pineapple and teriyaki sauce, lemon and garlic, or Cajun, ranch, or taco seasoning.

Per serving: Calories: 194; Total fat: 13g; Saturated fat: 8g; Cholesterol: 173mg; Sodium: 834mg; Carbohydrates: 4g; Fiber: 0g; Protein: 16g

THAI-STYLE SHRIMP STIR-FRY

FAMILY FAVORITE

Serves 4 / Prep Time: 15 minutes / Fry Time: 15 minutes

Thai cuisine is known for its lightness, as well as spices that pack heat into every bite. Featuring fresh vegetables and a fiery sauce, this meal is one of the fastest you can get on the dinner table.

8 ounces fresh green beans
6 mini bell peppers, thinly sliced
2 tablespoons olive oil
1 pound jumbo raw shrimp, peeled and deveined
½ cup Thai stir-fry sauce
1 tablespoon minced garlic
2 cups cooked jasmine or white rice
¼ cup shredded Thai basil

1. In an air fryer–safe pan, toss together the green beans, peppers, and olive oil until evenly coated.
2. Cook at 350°F for 5 minutes.
3. Add the shrimp, stir, and cook for another 5 minutes.
4. Add the stir-fry sauce and garlic, stir, and cook for another 5 minutes.
5. Serve over rice with a sprinkle of Thai basil on top.

Change It Up: Instead of serving with rice, try mixing this stir-fry into noodles.

Per serving: Calories: 321; Total fat: 8g; Saturated fat: 1g; Cholesterol: 143mg; Sodium: 965mg; Carbohydrates: 39g; Fiber: 3g; Protein: 22g

CRAB CAKES

FAMILY FAVORITE

Serves 4 / Prep Time: 10 minutes, plus 1 hour to refrigerate / Fry Time: 20 minutes

Crab cakes are a classic, comforting way to get your seafood fix with a bit of extra crunch. This version uses panko bread crumbs, which crisp up nicely. Enjoy this recipe as an appetizer, as a main dish paired with a salad or roasted vegetables, or as the protein in a hearty sandwich. Serve with Tartar Sauce ([here](#)) or rémoulade.

2 large eggs
2 tablespoons mayonnaise
1 teaspoon Dijon mustard
1 teaspoon Worcestershire sauce
1½ teaspoons Old Bay seasoning
¼ cup finely chopped scallions
1 pound lump crabmeat
½ cup panko bread crumbs
Oil, for spraying
1 lemon, cut into wedges

1. In a large bowl, mix together the eggs, mayonnaise, mustard, Worcestershire sauce, Old Bay, and scallions.
2. Add the crabmeat and bread crumbs and fold gently until combined, taking care not to break up the crab chunks too much.
3. Cover with plastic wrap and refrigerate for at least 1 hour.

4. Preheat the air fryer to 350°F. Line the air fryer basket with parchment and spray lightly with oil.
5. Divide the mixture into 8 equal portions and shape into 1-inch-thick patties, taking care not to pack too tightly. Place 4 patties in the prepared basket and spray lightly with oil.
6. Cook for 5 minutes, flip, spray with oil again, and cook for another 5 minutes, until golden brown and crispy. Repeat with the remaining patties.
7. Squeeze a lemon wedge over each crab cake.

Change It Up: These crab cakes are also great with hot sauce, taco or ranch seasoning, grated Parmesan cheese, or shredded cheddar cheese—just add the ingredients before refrigerating. You can also make this recipe with frozen crab. Thaw for 10 minutes at room temperature so you can mix it like fresh.

Per serving: Calories: 224; Total fat: 10g; Saturated fat: 2g; Cholesterol: 184mg; Sodium: 589mg; Carbohydrates: 6g; Fiber: 1g; Protein: 25g

Would you like to write for Sonicbond Publishing?

At Sonicbond Publishing we are always on the look-out for authors, particularly for our two main series:

On Track. Mixing fact with in depth analysis, the On Track series examines the work of a particular musical artist or group. All genres are considered from easy listening and jazz to 60s soul to 90s pop, via rock and metal.

On Screen. This series looks at the world of film and television. Subjects considered include directors, actors and writers, as well as entire television and film series. As with the On Track series, we balance fact with analysis.

While professional writing experience would, of course, be an advantage the most important qualification is to have real enthusiasm and knowledge of your subject. First-time authors are welcomed, but the ability to write well in English is essential.

Sonicbond Publishing has distribution throughout Europe and North America, and all books are also published in E-book form. Authors will be paid a royalty based on sales of their book.

Further details are available from www.sonicbondpublishing.co.uk. To contact us, complete the contact form there or email info@sonicbondpublishing.co.uk

Also from Sonicbond Publishing

On Track series
Queen Andrew Wild 978-1-78952-003-3
Emerson Lake and Palmer Mike Goode 978-1-78952-000-2
Deep Purple and Rainbow 1968-79 Steve Pilkington 978-1-78952-002-6
Yes Stephen Lambe 978-1-78952-001-9
Blue Oyster Cult Jacob Holm-Lupo 978-1-78952-007-1
The Beatles Andrew Wild 978-1-78952-009-5
Roy Wood and the Move James R Turner 978-1-78952-008-8
Genesis Stuart MacFarlane 978-1-78952-005-7
Jethro Tull Jordan Blum 978-1-78952-016-3
The Rolling Stones 1963-80 Steve Pilkington 978-1-78952-017-0
Judas Priest John Tucker 978-1-78952-018-7
Toto Jacob Holm-Lupo 978-1-78952-019-4
Van Der Graaf Generator Dan Coffey 978-1-78952-031-6
Frank Zappa 1966 to 1979 Eric Benac 978-1-78952-033-0
Elton John in the 1970s Peter Kearns 978-1-78952-034-7
The Moody Blues Geoffrey Feakes 978-1-78952-042-2
The Beatles Solo 1969-1980 Andrew Wild 978-1-78952-042-2
Steely Dan Jez Rowden 978-1-78952-043-9

On Screen series
Carry On... Stephen Lambe 978-1-78952-004-0
Audrey Hepburn Ellen Cheshire 978-1-78952-011-8
Powell and Pressburger Sam Proctor 978-1-78952-013-2
Seinfeld Seasons 1 to 5 Stephen Lambe 978-1-78952-012-5
Francis Ford Coppola Stephen Lambe 978-1-78952-022-4

Other Books
Not As Good As The Book Andy Tillison 978-1-78952-021-7
The Voice. Frank Sinatra in the 1940s
Stephen Lambe 978-1-78952-032-3

and many more to come!

CLASSIC FRENCH MUSSELS

FAMILY FAVORITE
GLUTEN-FREE
SUPER-FAST

Serves 4 / Prep Time: 5 minutes / Fry Time: 8 minutes

Mussels are a delicacy synonymous with cozy French bistros. Traditionally cooked on the stovetop, they may seem complicated and time-consuming. But this is one of the easiest recipes for the air fryer—the tender mollusks will be ready in less than 15 minutes.

Oil, for spraying
1 pound blue mussels
1 tablespoon unsalted butter
2 teaspoons minced garlic
1 teaspoon dried chives
1 teaspoon dried basil
1 teaspoon dried parsley
1 cup water
Lemon wedges, for garnish

1. Line the air fryer basket with parchment and spray lightly with oil.
2. Run the mussels under cold water and, using a clean scrub brush, remove any debris. Lightly tap any open shells and toss those that don't close.
3. In a microwave-safe bowl, combine the butter, garlic, chives, basil, parsley, and water. Microwave on high for 30 to 40 seconds, or until the butter is melted. Stir to combine and reserve half of the sauce in a small bowl.
4. Add the mussels to the remaining sauce and toss to coat.
5. Place the mussels in the prepared basket, taking care not to overcrowd. You may need to work in batches, depending on the size of your air fryer.
6. Cook at 390°F for 4 minutes, stir, and cook for another 4 minutes, or until the mussels have opened. Discard any that do not open.
7. Transfer to a serving bowl, drizzle with the reserved sauce, and garnish with lemon wedges.

Fry Fact: Fresh mussels should smell like the sea and the shells should be tightly closed. They are best eaten the same day you buy them, but you can store them in the refrigerator for up to 2 days before cooking.

Per serving: Calories: 53; Total fat: 4g; Saturated fat: 2g; Cholesterol: 16mg; Sodium: 104mg; Carbohydrates: 2g; Fiber: 0g; Protein: 4g

HOT CRAB DIP

FAMILY FAVORITE
GLUTEN-FREE

Serves 8 / Prep Time: 5 minutes / Fry Time: 12 minutes

Gracing holiday party buffet tables for decades, this thick and creamy melted cheese dip is loaded with lump crabmeat and bursting with flavor. You can air fry this dip in less than 20 minutes. Serve it with crackers or crostini or, for a healthier option, sliced peppers or carrots.

Oil, for spraying
4 ounces cream cheese, at room temperature
¼ cup sour cream
¼ cup mayonnaise
8 ounces lump crabmeat, fresh or frozen and thawed
½ cup shredded cheddar cheese
1 tablespoon dry Italian seasoning
1 teaspoon finely chopped fresh parsley (optional)

1. Line an air fryer–safe ramekin or casserole-style dish with parchment and spray lightly with oil.
2. In a small bowl, mix together the cream cheese, sour cream, and mayonnaise. Fold in the crabmeat, cheese, and Italian seasoning. Transfer to the prepared ramekin.
3. Cook at 320°F for 12 minutes.
4. Sprinkle with the parsley (if using) and serve warm.

Change It Up: For different flavor combinations, swap in pepper Jack, brie, or Colby-Jack cheese, as well as lobster or shrimp. Also try sliced mushrooms, chopped artichoke hearts, minced onions, chopped green bell peppers, or minced garlic.

Per serving: Calories: 162; Total fat: 14g; Saturated fat: 6g; Cholesterol: 52mg; Sodium: 227mg; Carbohydrates: 1g; Fiber: 0g; Protein: 8g

CAN YOU FRY IT?

FROZEN CLAM STRIPS

Preheat the air fryer to 400°F. Line the air fryer basket with parchment and spray lightly with oil. Put the clams in the prepared basket. Cook for 12 to 15 minutes, shaking after 5 minutes, or until crispy.

10-MINUTE GARLIC PESTO SCALLOPS

GLUTEN-FREE
SUPER-FAST

Serves 4 / Prep Time: 5 minutes / Fry Time: 5 minutes

Low in fat and high in protein, omega-3 fatty acids, vitamin B12, calcium, and iron, scallops pack a punch when it comes to nutrition. You can make these in less than 15 minutes in the air fryer, and they're the perfect accompaniment to buttered angel hair pasta.

Oil, for spraying
¼ cup basil pesto
3 tablespoons heavy cream
1 tablespoon olive oil
2 teaspoons minced garlic
1 teaspoon salt
½ teaspoon freshly ground black pepper
1 pound sea scallops

1. Line the air fryer basket with parchment and spray lightly with oil.
2. In a small saucepan, combine the pesto, heavy cream, olive oil, garlic, salt, and black pepper and bring to a simmer over medium heat, stirring occasionally. Cook for 2 minutes and set aside.
3. Place the scallops in the prepared basket.

4. Cook at 320°F for 5 minutes, flipping after 3 minutes to ensure both sides cook evenly.
5. Transfer to a serving dish, pour the pesto sauce over the top, and serve.

Change It Up: Instead of pesto, serve the scallops in a lemon butter sauce, over cauliflower risotto, in a Tuscan sundried tomato sauce, sprinkled with panko bread crumbs, on top of sweet corn and chopped chiles, or brushed with a teriyaki glaze.

Per serving: Calories: 232; Total fat: 17g; Saturated fat: 5g; Cholesterol: 45mg; Sodium: 1170mg; Carbohydrates: 5g; Fiber: 0g; Protein: 16g

CRISPY FRIED CALAMARI

Serves 4 / Prep Time: 10 minutes / Fry Time: 8 minutes

Tender calamari is traditionally battered and breaded before being deep-fried. This version has just a light coating of flour, which cuts nearly 90 percent of the calories but absolutely none of the taste.

Oil, for spraying
¼ cup all-purpose flour
2 teaspoons salt, plus more if desired
2 teaspoons freshly ground black pepper
1 large egg
1 pound calamari, cut into rings

1. Preheat the air fryer to 350°F. Line the air fryer basket with parchment and spray lightly with oil.
2. Combine the flour, salt, and black pepper in a zip-top plastic bag and set aside.
3. In a medium bowl, whisk the egg. Add the calamari and turn to coat evenly.
4. Transfer the calamari to the zip-top bag, seal, and shake well until evenly coated.
5. Place the calamari in the prepared basket and spray lightly with oil.
6. Cook for 5 minutes, flip, spray with oil, and cook for another 3 minutes, until crispy and cooked through.
7. Sprinkle with additional salt, if desired, and serve.

Pair It With: For added flavor, dip the calamari in marinara sauce or chipotle mayonnaise. Serve as part of an appetizer sampler platter alongside Soft Pretzel Bites, Fried Pickle Chips, and Mozzarella Balls.

Fry Fact: You can make this recipe with frozen calamari, too. Thaw first by running them under cool water for several minutes.

Per serving: Calories: 161; Total fat: 4g; Saturated fat: 1g; Cholesterol: 311mg; Sodium: 649mg; Carbohydrates: 10g; Fiber: 0g; Protein: 20g

CHAPTER 6
POULTRY

Honey-Glazed Chicken Thighs
Barbecue Chicken Breast
Coconut Chicken Tenders
Chicken Parmesan Classic
Whole Chicken
Sriracha-Honey Chicken Nuggets
Sesame Chicken   Sweet
and Sour Chicken Chicken
Potstickers   Ultimate Spicy
Chicken Sandwich Crispy Lemon
Pepper Chicken Breast Jalapeño
Popper Hasselback Chicken Juicy
Paprika Chicken Breast Chicken
Enchiladas   Easy Chicken
Nachos Chicken Cordon Bleu
Chicken Fajitas
Hawaiian-Style Chicken
Thighs Cornish Game Hens
Herb Butter Turkey Breast

CHICKEN FAJITAS

HONEY-GLAZED CHICKEN THIGHS

FAMILY FAVORITE

Serves 4 / Prep Time: 5 minutes / Fry Time: 14 minutes

Chicken thighs are juicier, more tasty, and frequently more affordable than chicken bosoms. Coat them with a tacky sweet combo of soy sauce, vinegar, honey, garlic, and ginger, and you have an overwhelming dinner that sets pleasantly with rice and steamed vegetables.

Oil, for spraying
4 boneless, skinless chicken thighs, fat managed
3 tablespoons soy sauce
1 tablespoon balsamic vinegar
2 teaspoons honey
2 teaspoons minced garlic
1 teaspoon ground ginger

1. Preheat the air fryer to 400°F. Line the air fryer container with material and shower delicately with oil.
2. Place the chicken in the arranged basket.
3. Cook for 7 minutes, flip, and cook for an additional 7 minutes, or until the inside temperature arrives at 165°F and the juices run clear.
4. In a little pot, join the soy sauce, balsamic vinegar, honey, garlic, and ginger and cook over low hotness for 1 to 2 minutes, until warmed through.
5. Transfer the chicken to a serving plate and sprinkle with the sauce not long before serving.

Change It Up: Instead of the honey coating, brush the thighs with your beloved grill sauce.

Per serving: Calories: 257; Total fat: 8g; Saturated fat: 2g; Cholesterol: 181mg; Sodium: 844mg; Carbohydrates: 5g; Fiber: 0g; Protein: 39g

BARBECUE CHICKEN BITES

FAMILY FAVORITE

Serves 4/Prep Time: 5 minutes/Fry Time: 19 minutes

Lightly floured to add a touch of fresh under the sauce, these chicken nibbles fulfill a similar wanting as grill wings, however you don't need to manage profound broiling or muddled bones. These chomps make an incredible tidbit for game day, yet they are comparable for a weeknight supper when combined with some vegetables.

Oil, for spraying
2 (6-ounce) boneless, skinless chicken bosoms, cut into reduced down pieces
½ cup generally useful flour
1 tablespoon granulated garlic
2 teaspoons prepared salt
1 cup grill sauce

1. Line the air fryer container with material and splash daintily with oil.
2. Place the chicken, flour, garlic, and prepared salt in a zip-top plastic pack, seal, and shake well until equally coated.
3. Place the chicken in an even layer in the pre-arranged bin and shower generously with oil. You might have to work in clusters, contingent upon the size of your air fryer.
4. Cook at 390°F for 8 minutes, flip, splash with more oil, and cook for an additional 8 minutes, or until the interior temperature arrives at 165°F and the juices run clear.
5. Transfer the chicken to a huge bowl and throw with the grill sauce.
6. Line the air fryer bushel with new material, return the chicken to the bin, and cook for another 3 minutes.

Change It Up: Serve the chicken in sliders with coleslaw, in pita pockets, or stuffed into tacos.

Per serving: Calories: 228; Total fat: 3g; Saturated fat: 1g; Cholesterol: 52mg; Sodium: 921mg; Carbohydrates: 30g; Fiber: 1g; Protein: 18g

COCONUT CHICKEN TENDERS

FAMILY FAVORITE

Serves 4/Prep Time: 10 minutes/Fry Time: 12 minutes

Juicy chicken strips enclosed by firm, somewhat sweet chipped coconut make an ideal child cordial weeknight feast or a fast party canapé. These air-singed tenders have 90% less fat than their southern style partners and invest in some opportunity to cook.

Oil, for splashing
2 enormous eggs
¼ cup milk
1 tablespoon hot sauce
1½ cups improved chipped coconut
¾ cup panko bread pieces 1
teaspoon salt
½ teaspoon newly ground dark pepper 1
pound chicken tenders

1. Line the air fryer container with material and shower gently with oil.
2. In a little bowl, whisk together the eggs, milk, and hot sauce.
3. In a shallow dish, combine as one the coconut, bread morsels, salt, and dark pepper.
4. Coat the chicken in the egg blend, then, at that point, dig in the coconut combination until equitably coated.
5. Place the chicken in the pre-arranged crate and shower generously with oil.
6. Cook at 400°F for 6 minutes, flip, splash with more oil, and cook for an additional 6 minutes, or until the inward temperature arrives at 165°F.

Change It Up: Try covering the chicken with squashed corn drops rather than coconut and panko bread scraps, or add farm or taco preparing to the bread morsels rather than coconut.

Per serving: Calories: 302; Total fat: 13g; Saturated fat: 9g; Cholesterol: 107mg; Sodium: 795mg; Carbohydrates: 17g; Fiber: 1g; Protein: 29g

CHICKEN PARMESAN

FAMILY FAVORITE

Serves 4/Prep Time: 15 minutes/Fry Time: 10 minutes

What's more fulfilling than succulent chicken bosom covered in firm bread

scraps and canvassed in marinara and Parmesan cheddar? It's a sample of Italy comfortable, and prepared in a fraction of the time than if you heated it.

Oil, for spraying
2 (8-ounce) boneless, skinless chicken bosoms
1 cup Italian-style bread crumbs
¼ cup ground Parmesan cheddar, in addition to ½ cup destroyed 4 tablespoons unsalted spread, melted
½ cup marinara sauce

1. Preheat the air fryer to 360°F. Line the air fryer bin with material and shower daintily with oil.
2. Cut every chicken bosom in half through its thickness to make 4 meager cutlets. Utilizing a meat tenderizer, pound every cutlet until it is about ¾ inch thick.
3. On a plate, combine as one the bread morsels and ground Parmesan cheese.
4. Lightly brush the chicken with the softened spread, then, at that point, dunk into the bread scrap mixture.
5. Place the chicken in the pre-arranged bin and splash daintily with oil. You might have to work in clusters, contingent upon the size of your air fryer.
6. Cook for 6 minutes. Top the chicken with the marinara and destroyed Parmesan cheddar, partitioning equitably. Cook for one more 3 to 4 minutes, or until brilliant brown, fresh, and the inward temperature arrives at 165°F.

Pair It With: Try this dish with Garlic-Parmesan Crispy Baby Potatoes or Parmesan Mushrooms.

Per serving: Calories: 351; Total fat: 17g; Saturated fat: 9g; Cholesterol: 119mg; Sodium: 407mg; Carbohydrates: 17g; Fiber: 1g; Protein: 30g

CLASSIC WHOLE CHICKEN

GLUTEN-FREE
FAMILY FAVORITE

Serves 4/Prep Time: 5 minutes/Fry Time: 50 minutes

There's nothing more consoling on the supper table than a simmered entire chicken. But preparing it in the oven takes 1 hour 30 minutes or more. This chicken feeds the family in under 60 minutes, and it comes out wonderful each time.

Oil, for spraying
1 (4-pound) entire chicken, giblets eliminated 1 tablespoon olive oil
1 teaspoon paprika
½ teaspoon granulated garlic
½ teaspoon salt
½ teaspoon newly ground dark pepper
¼ teaspoon finely slashed new parsley, for garnish

1. Line the air fryer bushel with material and shower daintily with oil.
2. Pat the chicken dry with paper towels. Rub it with the olive oil until equitably coated.
3. In a little bowl, combine as one the paprika, garlic, salt, and dark pepper and sprinkle it uniformly over the chicken.
4. Place the chicken in the pre-arranged bushel, bosom side down.
5. Cook at 360°F for 30 minutes, flip, and cook for an additional 20 minutes, or until the inside temperature arrives at 165°F and the juices run clear.
6. Sprinkle with the parsley before serving.

Change It Up: Try brushing a layer of teriyaki or balsamic coating over the chicken when 5 minutes of cooking time remain.

Per serving: Calories: 625; Total fat: 45g; Saturated fat: 12g; Cholesterol: 207mg; Sodium: 484mg; Carbohydrates: 0g; Fiber: 0g; Protein: 51g

SRIRACHA-HONEY CHICKEN NUGGETS

FAMILY FAVORITE

Serves 6/Prep Time: 15 minutes/Fry Time: 19 minutes

The red hot kind of sriracha gives the engaging hotness in these chicken tenders, which is adjusted by some pleasantness from honey and a smidgen of sugar. They're so want commendable, you will not contemplate an excursion to the drive-through.

Oil, for splashing
1 enormous egg
¾ cup milk
1 cup universally handy flour
2 tablespoons confectioners' sugar
½ teaspoon paprika
½ teaspoon salt
½ teaspoon newly ground dark pepper
2 boneless, skinless chicken bosoms, cut into scaled down pieces
½ cup grill sauce 2
tablespoons honey
1 tablespoon sriracha

1. Line the air fryer container with material and shower delicately with oil.
2. In a little bowl, whisk together the egg and milk.
3. In a medium bowl, consolidate the flour, confectioners' sugar, paprika, salt, and dark pepper and stir.
4. Coat the chicken in the egg blend, then, at that point, dig in the flour combination until equitably coated.
5. Place the chicken in the pre-arranged crate and shower generously with oil.
6. Cook at 390°F for 8 minutes, flip, shower with more oil, and cook for one more 6 to 8 minutes, or until the inside temperature arrives at 165°F

    and the juices run clear.
7. In a huge bowl, combine as one the grill sauce, honey, and sriracha.
8. Transfer the chicken to the bowl and throw until all around covered with the grill sauce mixture.
9. Line the air fryer bushel with new material, return the chicken to the bin, and cook for one more 2 to 3 minutes, until carmelized and crispy.

Pair It With: Serve with Fried Pickle Chips and Jalapeño Poppers.

Per serving: Calories: 205; Total fat: 4g; Saturated fat: 1g; Cholesterol: 69mg; Sodium: 485mg; Carbohydrates: 27g; Fiber: 1g; Protein: 14g

SESAME CHICKEN

FAMILY FAVORITE

Serves 6/Prep Time: 10 minutes/Fry Time: 18 minutes

You needn't bother with a wok for this simple interpretation of the Chinese eatery exemplary. Feed the entire family quicker than it takes to get conveyance, and at a much lower cost. You'll likewise be killing up to 90 percent of the fat and calories. Serve on a bed of white rice close by steamed vegetables.

Oil, for spraying
2 (6-ounce) boneless, skinless chicken bosoms, cut into reduced down pieces
½ cup cornstarch, in addition to 1 tablespoon
¼ cup soy sauce
2 tablespoons pressed light earthy colored sugar 2 tablespoons pineapple juice
1 tablespoon molasses
½ teaspoon ground ginger
1 tablespoon water
2 teaspoons sesame seeds

1. Line the air fryer crate with material and shower delicately with oil.
2. Place the chicken and ½ cup of cornstarch in a zip-top plastic pack, seal, and shake well until equitably coated.
3. Place the chicken in an even layer in the pre-arranged bushel and splash generously with oil. You might have to work in clumps, contingent upon the size of your fryer.
4. Cook at 390°F for 9 minutes, flip, splash with more oil, and cook for one more 8 to 9 minutes, or until the inside temperature arrives at 165°F.
5. In a little pan, join the soy sauce, earthy colored sugar, pineapple juice, molasses, and ginger over medium hotness and cook, mixing habitually, until the earthy colored sugar has dissolved.
6. In a little bowl, combine as one the water and staying 1 tablespoon of cornstarch. Empty it into the soy sauce mixture.
7. Bring the combination to a bubble, mixing as often as possible, until the sauce thickens. Eliminate from the heat.

8. Transfer the chicken to an enormous bowl, add the sauce, and throw until equally covered. Sprinkle with the sesame seeds and serve.

Pair It With: Serve with Asiago Shishito Peppers as an appetizer and finish with Apple Pie Egg Rolls for dessert.

Per serving: Calories: 143; Total fat: 3g; Saturated fat: 0g; Cholesterol: 34mg; Sodium: 464mg; Carbohydrates: 18g; Fiber: 0g; Protein: 12g

SWEET AND SOUR CHICKEN

FAMILY FAVORITE

Serves 4/Prep Time: 10 minutes/Fry Time: 23 minutes

Instead of attempting to view as the ideal Chinese takeout, why not make your own? The air fryer cuts the cooking time and you don't need to remain over a hot pot of oil.

FOR THE CHICKEN

Oil, for spraying
6 boneless, skinless chicken thighs, cut into reduced down pieces
½ cup cornstarch
1 (8-ounce) can pineapple goodies, drained
1 green chime pepper, cultivated and cut into 1-inch pieces
¼ sweet onion, cut into 1-inch pieces

FOR THE SWEET AND SOUR SAUCE

½ cup sugar
3 tablespoons vinegar
⅓ cup water, in addition to 1 tablespoon 1 tablespoon ketchup
1½ tablespoons cornstarch

FOR SERVING

Cooked white rice

TO MAKE THE CHICKEN

1. Line the air fryer bin with material and splash softly with oil.
2. Combine the chicken and cornstarch in a zip-top plastic pack, seal, and shake well until equitably coated.
3. Place the chicken in an even layer in the pre-arranged crate and

shower generously with oil. You might have to work in clumps, contingent upon the size of your air fryer.

4. Cook at 390°F for 9 minutes, flip, splash with more oil, and cook for one more 8 to 9 minutes, or until the inward temperature arrives at 165°F

   and the juices run clear.

5. Add the pineapple, ringer pepper, and onion to the container, throw to join, and cook for another 5 minutes.

TO MAKE THE SWEET AND SOUR SAUCE

6. In a little pan, consolidate the sugar, vinegar, and ⅓ cup of water over medium hotness and cook, mixing every now and again, until the sugar has disintegrated. Add the ketchup and mix to combine.

7. In a little bowl, combine as one the cornstarch and staying 1 tablespoon of water and empty it into the sauce combination. Cook for 30 seconds, mixing often, until it thickens.

TO SERVE

8. Transfer the chicken combination to an enormous bowl, add the sauce, and throw until uniformly covered. Spoon the rice into bowls and top with the chicken mixture.

Faster Frying: You can utilize locally acquired prepared sauce as opposed to making your own. Or on the other hand utilize frozen chicken tenders and cook them at 400°F for 12 minutes.

Per serving: Calories: 696; Total fat: 30g; Saturated fat: 8g; Cholesterol: 167mg; Sodium: 183mg; Carbohydrates: 74g; Fiber: 2g; Protein: 31g

CAN YOU FRY IT?

CHICKEN WINGS

Line the air fryer basket with parchment and spray lightly with oil. Place the chicken wings in the prepared basket. Cook at 380°F for 25 minutes, tossing every 5 minutes. Increase the heat to 400°F and cook for another 5 to 8 minutes, or until the skin is golden and crispy.

CHICKEN POTSTICKERS

FAMILY FAVORITE

Serves 4/Prep Time: 15 minutes/Fry Time: 6 minutes

Steamed Asian-style dumplings loaded down with meat and vegetables and plunged in sauce are an enormous group pleaser for all ages. When cooked in the air fryer, the wonton coverings get firm while the internal parts stay sodden and flavorful.

Oil, for spraying
6 ounces finely slashed rotisserie chicken
¼ cup finely hacked scallions
1 tablespoon dried minced onions
2 teaspoons soy sauce
1½ teaspoons rice vinegar
½ teaspoon minced garlic
½ teaspoon ground ginger
16 square wonton wrappers
<u>Sweet and Sour Sauce</u>

1. Line the air fryer crate with material and shower softly with oil.
2. Pour some water into a little bowl.
3. In a medium bowl, combine as one the chicken, scallions, onions, soy sauce, rice vinegar, garlic, and ginger.
4. Working in little clusters, spread out the wonton coverings on a work surface.
5. Place 1 tablespoon of the chicken blend in the focal point of each wrapper.
6. Using your finger, soak the edges of the wonton covering with water and crease into a triangle. Press the edges to seal. Rehash with the excess wrappers.
7. Place the potstickers in a solitary layer in the pre-arranged crate and splash generously with oil. You might have to work in bunches, contingent upon the size of your air fryer.
8. Cook at 400°F for 5 to 6 minutes, or until brilliant brown and crispy.
9. Serve hot with the sauce as an afterthought for dipping.

Faster Frying: You can cook frozen potstickers at 400°F for 8 minutes.

Per serving: Calories: 160; Total fat: 2g; Saturated fat: 0g; Cholesterol: 39mg; Sodium: 469mg; Carbohydrates: 20g; Fiber: 1g; Protein: 15g

ULTIMATE SPICY CHICKEN

SANDWICH

FAMILY FAVORITE

Serves 4/Prep Time: 15 minutes, in addition to 30 minutes to marinate/Fry Time: 22 minutes

Spicy chicken sandwiches are largely the fury, however now and again you would rather not sit tight in line for the most recent cheap food version. This rendition is just as great, and a ton better. Assemble your fantasy sandwich with trimmings like cheddar, mayonnaise, hot sauce, tomato, lettuce, coleslaw, and pickles.

Oil, for spraying
2 (6-ounce) boneless, skinless chicken bosoms
1½ cups pickle juice
1½ cups universally handy flour
2 tablespoons confectioners' sugar
½ teaspoon paprika
½ teaspoon salt
½ teaspoon newly ground dark pepper 2 enormous eggs
1 cup milk
4 burger buns
Sandwich trimmings, like lettuce, tomato, onion, and sauce of choice

1. Line the air fryer bushel with material and splash daintily with oil.
2. Cut every chicken bosom in half through its thickness to make 4 slender cutlets. Utilizing a meat tenderizer, pound every cutlet until it is about ¾ inch thick.
3. Place the chicken and the pickle juice in a zip-top plastic sack, seal, and refrigerate for something like 30 minutes.
4. In a shallow bowl, combine as one the flour, confectioners' sugar, paprika, salt, and dark pepper.
5. In a little bowl, whisk together the eggs and milk.
6. Coat the chicken in the egg combination, then, at that point, dig it in the flour blend until equally coated.
7. Place the chicken in an even layer in the pre-arranged crate and splash generously with oil. You might have to work in clusters, contingent upon the size of your air fryer.
8. Cook at 400°F for 11 minutes, flip, shower with more oil, and cook for one more 8 to 11 minutes, or until brilliant brown and the

interior temperature arrives at 165°F.
9. Cut every chicken cutlet into equal parts and gather the sandwiches on the buns with the ideal fixings.

Per serving: Calories: 349; Total fat: 7g; Saturated fat: 2g; Cholesterol: 137mg; Sodium: 632mg; Carbohydrates: 43g; Fiber: 2g; Protein: 26g

CRISPY LEMON PEPPER CHICKEN BREAST

FAMILY FAVORITE

Serves 4/Prep Time: 5 minutes/Fry Time: 30 minutes

Lemon pepper is an extraordinary method for including some punch without heaping additional fat or carbs. Serve this tasty chicken with a green plate of mixed greens and some chilled tea for an ideal warm-climate meal.

Oil, for spraying
4 (6-ounce) boneless, skinless chicken bosoms
1 tablespoon lemon pepper
1½ teaspoons granulated garlic
1 teaspoon salt
4 tablespoons panko bread crumbs

1. Preheat the air fryer to 360°F. Line the air fryer crate with material and shower daintily with oil.
2. Place the chicken in the pre-arranged bushel and season with the lemon pepper, garlic, and salt. You might have to work in clumps, contingent upon the size of your air fryer.
3. Cook for 15 minutes, flip, and cook for an additional 13 minutes, or until the inner temperature arrives at 165°F.
4. Sprinkle the bread pieces on top, shower softly with oil, and cook for one more 1 to 2 minutes, until the covering is crisp.

Change It Up: You can utilize sans gluten panko or skip it through and through. Attempt prepared salt, poultry, or jerk preparing for a difference in pace.

Per serving: Calories: 148; Total fat: 4g; Saturated fat: 1g; Cholesterol: 83mg; Sodium: 533mg; Carbohydrates: 0g; Fiber: 0g; Protein: 26g

JALAPEÑO POPPER HASSELBACK CHICKEN

GLUTEN-FREE

Serves 2/Prep Time: 10 minutes/Fry Time: 19 minutes

In this formula, we cut the chicken bosoms on various occasions partially through and stuff each cut with bacon, cheddar, and jalapeños before air singing flawlessly. The outcome looks perfect and tastes even better.

Oil, for spraying
2 (8-ounce) boneless, skinless chicken bosoms
2 ounces cream cheddar, softened
¼ cup bacon bits
¼ cup cleaved salted jalapeños
½ cup destroyed cheddar, divided

1. Line the air fryer container with material and splash delicately with oil.
2. Make different cuts across the highest point of every chicken bosom, cutting just most of the way through.
3. In a medium bowl, combine as one the cream cheddar, bacon bits, jalapeños, and ¼ cup of cheddar. Spoon a portion of the blend into each cut.
4. Place the chicken in the arranged basket.
5. Cook at 350°F for 14 minutes. Disperse the excess ¼ cup of cheddar on top of the chicken and cook for one more 2 to 5 minutes, or until the cheddar is dissolved and the interior temperature arrives at 165°F.

Change It Up: Stuff the chicken with cheddar and cleaved broccoli, ham and Swiss cheddar, spinach and provolone cheddar, or bacon, cheddar, and grill sauce.

Per serving: Calories: 568; Total fat: 31g; Saturated fat: 14g; Cholesterol: 243mg; Sodium: 678mg; Carbohydrates: 3g; Fiber: 0g; Protein: 65g

JUICY PAPRIKA CHICKEN

BREAST

**FAMILY FAVORITE
GLUTEN-FREE**

Serves 4/Prep Time: 5 minutes/Fry Time: 30 minutes

This delicate paprika-prepared chicken gives you that incredible barbecued surface you ache for, with no charcoal or propane required.

Oil, for spraying
4 (6-ounce) boneless, skinless chicken bosoms
1 tablespoon olive oil
1 tablespoon paprika
1 tablespoon pressed light brown sugar
½ teaspoon cayenne pepper
½ teaspoon onion powder
½ teaspoon granulated garlic

1. Line the air fryer crate with material and splash softly with oil.
2. Brush the chicken with the olive oil.
3. In a little bowl, combine as one the paprika, earthy colored sugar, cayenne pepper, onion powder, and garlic and sprinkle it over the chicken.
4. Place the chicken in the pre-arranged bushel. You might have to work in bunches, contingent upon the size of your air fryer.
5. Cook at 360°F for 15 minutes, flip, and cook for an additional 15 minutes, or until the inside temperature arrives at 165°F. Serve immediately.

Change It Up: Season the chicken with lemon pepper or brush with Italian plate of mixed greens dressing or grill sauce.

Per serving: Calories: 161; Total fat: 4g; Saturated fat: 8g; Cholesterol: 83mg; Sodium: 53mg; Carbohydrates: 3g; Fiber: 1g; Protein: 26g

CAN YOU FRY IT?

FROZEN CHICKEN

Preheat the air fryer to 390°F. Line the air fryer basket with parchment and spray lightly with oil. Place the frozen chicken breast in the prepared basket and cook for 20 to 25 minutes.

CHICKEN ENCHILADAS

FAMILY FAVORITE

Serves 4/Prep Time: 10 minutes/Fry Time: 8 minutes

Enchiladas probably won't be the primary thing you think to cook in an air fryer, however they are so natural and fast, you'll need to add this formula to your customary pivot. Use leftover Juicy Paprika Chicken Breast or rotisserie chicken.

Oil, for spraying
3 cups destroyed cooked chicken
1 bundle taco seasoning
8 flour tortillas, at room temperature
½ cup canned dark beans, washed and depleted
1 (4-ounce) can diced green chiles, drained
1 (10-ounce) would red or green enchilada be able to sauce 1 cup destroyed cheddar cheese

1. Line the air fryer bushel with material and splash gently with oil. (Try not to avoid the progression of covering the crate; the material will hold the sauce and cheddar back from dribbling through the holes.)
2. In a little bowl, combine as one the chicken and taco seasoning.
3. Divide the blend among the tortillas. Top with the dark beans and green chiles. Cautiously roll up each tortilla.
4. Place the enchiladas, crease side down, in the pre-arranged container. You might have to work in clusters, contingent upon the size of your air fryer.

5. Spoon the enchilada sauce over the enchiladas. Utilize barely sufficient sauce to hold them back from drying out. You can add more sauce when serving. Sprinkle the cheddar on top.
6. Cook at 360°F for 5 to 8 minutes, or until warmed through and the cheddar is melted.
7. Place 2 enchiladas on each plate and top with more enchilada sauce, if desired.

Change It Up: For an alternate flavor, add diced tomatoes or refried beans, use corn tortillas, or top with lettuce, sharp cream, and diced avocado after cooking.

Per serving: Calories: 506; Total fat: 19g; Saturated fat: 8g; Cholesterol: 107mg; Sodium: 859mg; Carbohydrates: 39g; Fiber: 4g; Protein: 43g

EASY CHICKEN NACHOS

FAMILY FAVORITE
GLUTEN-FREE
SUPER-FAST

Serves 8/Prep Time: 5 minutes/Fry Time: 5 minutes

Nachos are extraordinarily basic but then so adaptable. You can serve them as a hors d'oeuvre or a primary dish, and you can finish off them with fixings to fulfill pretty much any hankering. I like to make nachos when I have a couple of days of extras. In the event that you like the chicken-bacon-farm combo, you'll truly adore these.

Oil, for spraying
3 cups destroyed cooked chicken
1 (1-ounce) bundle farm seasoning
¼ cup sharp cream
2 cups corn tortilla chips
⅓ cup bacon bits
1 cup destroyed cheddar 1
tablespoon hacked scallions

1. Line the air fryer container with material and splash softly with oil.
2. In a little bowl, combine as one the chicken, farm preparing, and acrid cream.
3. Place the tortilla contributes the pre-arranged bin and top with the chicken combination. Add the bacon bits, cheddar, and scallions.

4. Cook at 425°F for 3 to 5 minutes, or until warmed through and the cheddar is melted.

Change It Up: Make customary nachos with beans, meat, cheddar, and taco fixings. Make pizza nachos with pasta sauce, cheddar, and child pepperoni, or have a go at adding cooked hotdog, anchovies, ham, pineapple, alfredo sauce, chime peppers, grill sauce, olives, or onions.

Per serving: Calories: 232; Total fat: 13g; Saturated fat: 5g; Cholesterol: 66mg; Sodium: 291mg; Carbohydrates: 6g; Fiber: 0g; Protein: 21g

CHICKEN CORDON BLEU

FAMILY FAVORITE

Serves 4/Prep Time: 15 minutes/Fry Time: 20 minutes

This wanton dish-chicken loaded down with ham and cheddar and canvassed in bread scraps is one of my better half's top picks, however I seldom made this is a direct result of the oil it requires and the wreck it makes. But this air-fried version is much healthier, and it keeps my kitchen cleaner, too.

Oil, for spraying
2 (8-ounce) boneless, skinless chicken bosoms
4 cuts Swiss cheese
4 cuts shop ham
¾ cup universally handy flour
1 enormous egg, gently
beaten 1 cup bread
crumbs
½ teaspoon salt
½ teaspoon newly ground dark pepper

1. Preheat the air fryer to 375°F. Line the air fryer container with material and shower delicately with oil.
2. Cut every chicken bosom in half through its thickness to make 4 flimsy cutlets. Utilizing a meat tenderizer, pound every cutlet until it is about ¾ inch thick.
3. Top every cutlet with a cheddar cut and afterward a ham cut. Roll up the chicken and secure with a toothpick to hold it closed.
4. Place the flour, beaten egg, and bread morsels in isolated bowls.
5. Coat every chicken roll in the flour, dunk in the egg, and dig in the bread pieces until equitably covered. Season with the salt and dark pepper.
6. Place the chicken rolls in the pre-arranged bin and splash with oil. You might have to work in clusters, contingent upon the size of your air fryer.
7. Cook for 10 minutes, flip, splash with more oil, and cook for an additional 10 minutes, or until brilliant brown and the inward temperature reaches
   165°F and the juices run clear.

Change It Up: Try utilizing panko bread pieces, which are crunchier than standard bread morsels, or supplanting the chicken with veal. You can likewise skirt the flour and brush the chicken with Dijon mustard prior to covering it with bread crumbs.

Per serving: Calories: 409; Total fat: 14g; Saturated fat: 6g; Cholesterol: 159mg; Sodium: 654mg; Carbohydrates: 26g; Fiber: 1g; Protein: 42g

CHICKEN FAJITAS

FAMILY FAVORITE
GLUTEN-FREE

Serves 4/Prep Time: 7 minutes/Fry Time: 20 minutes

No one will accept these hot chicken fajitas, made with ringer peppers and onions and served in warm tortillas, didn't come directly from a sizzling skillet. Top with cheddar, guacamole, or harsh cream.

Oil, for spraying
1 pound boneless, skinless chicken bosoms, daintily cut
2 chime peppers, cultivated and meagerly sliced
1 onion, daintily cut
1 tablespoon olive oil
2 teaspoons stew powder
1 teaspoon salt
1 teaspoon ground cumin
4 corn or flour tortillas, at room temperature
Assorted garnishes, like destroyed cheddar, guacamole, destroyed lettuce, slashed tomato, or acrid cream

1. Line the air fryer container with material and splash gently with oil.
2. Place the chicken, ringer peppers, onion, olive oil, bean stew powder, salt, and cumin in a zip-top plastic sack, seal, and shake until equitably covered. Move the combination to the arranged basket.
3. Cook at 360°F for 16 to 20 minutes, mixing following 10 minutes, until the inward temperature of the chicken arrives at 165°F and the juices run clear.
4. To warm the tortillas, stack them on a microwave-safe plate with a moist paper towel between every one and microwave for 30 to 60 seconds. Spoon the chicken blend on top and present with garnishes on the side.

Change It Up: Leftovers taste incredible on top of a serving of mixed greens. You can likewise transform this dish into a sautéed food by utilizing teriyaki sauce rather than bean stew powder and cumin and serving it over rice.

Per serving: Calories: 266; Total fat: 8g; Saturated fat: 1g; Cholesterol: 83mg; Sodium: 621mg; Carbohydrates: 21g; Fiber: 3g; Protein: 29g

HAWAIIAN-STYLE CHICKEN THIGHS

FAMILY FAVORITE

Serves 4/Prep Time: 7 minutes, in addition to 30 minutes to marinate/Fry Time: 15 minutes

You don't need to purchase a boarding pass to attempt this exemplary Hawaiian-enlivened dish. This improved on air-singed variant cooks significantly quicker yet at the same time packs in the flavor, praises of pineapple, soy sauce, and brown sugar.

Oil, for spraying
4 (6-ounce) boneless, skinless chicken thighs
1 (8-ounce) can pineapple lumps, depleted, ¼ cup juice reserved
¼ cup soy sauce
¼ cup pressed light earthy colored sugar 2 tablespoons ketchup
1 tablespoon minced garlic
2 teaspoons ground ginger

1. Line the air fryer bin with material and splash gently with oil.
2. Pierce the chicken thighs a few times with a fork and spot them in a zip-top plastic bag.
3. In a little bowl, whisk together the saved pineapple juice, soy sauce, earthy colored sugar, ketchup, garlic, and ginger.
4. Pour half of the sauce into the zip-top sack with the chicken, seal, and refrigerate for no less than 30 minutes.
5. Place the chicken in the pre-arranged container, saving the marinade.
6. Cook at 360°F for 7 minutes, flip, and cook for an additional 8 minutes, or until the inward temperature arrives at 165°F and the juices run clear.
7. Meanwhile, in a little pot over medium hotness, heat the marinade to the point of boiling, then, at that point, stew, blending much of the time, for 8 to 10 minutes, or until it thickens.
8. Top the chicken thighs with the pineapple pieces and sauce and serve.

Change It Up: This formula is incredible utilizing chicken fingers. Serve over white rice or in tacos.

Per serving: Calories: 192; Total fat: 5g; Saturated fat: 1g; Cholesterol: 107mg; Sodium: 589mg; Carbohydrates: 13g; Fiber: 1g; Protein: 23g

CORNISH GAME HENS

GLUTEN-FREE

Serves 2/Prep Time: 5 minutes/Fry Time: 45 minutes

Cornish game hens might sound intriguing, yet they are extraordinarily tasty and simple to find all things considered grocery stores. Make this super-simple air-singed form any time the hankering strikes.

Oil, for spraying
2 tablespoons olive oil
2 teaspoons salt
1 teaspoon granulated garlic
1 teaspoon paprika
1 teaspoon newly ground dark pepper
½ teaspoon dried basil
2 (2-pound) Cornish game hens

1. Line the air fryer container with material and shower delicately with oil.
2. In a little bowl, combine as one the olive oil, salt, garlic, paprika, dark pepper, and basil. Brush the blend all around the game hens.
3. Place the hens, bosom side down, in the arranged basket.
4. Cook at 360°F for 35 minutes, flip, and cook for an additional 10 minutes, or until the skin is fresh and the inward temperature arrives at 165°F.

Fry Fact: Even a more modest air fryer ought to have the option to fit 2 game hens. On the off chance that you have a bigger model, you can make 3 or 4 hens without changing the cooking time or temperature.

Per serving: Calories: 767; Total fat: 60g; Saturated fat: 15g; Cholesterol: 339mg; Sodium: 1069mg; Carbohydrates: 1g; Fiber: 1g; Protein: 57g

HERB BUTTER TURKEY BREAST

FAMILY FAVORITE
GLUTEN-FREE

Serves 4/Prep Time: 10 minutes/Fry Time: 1 hour

Use the air fryer to concoct a succulent, heavenly turkey bosom, and keep your stove allowed to make a side dish or dessert (or both!).

Oil, for spraying
1 (3-pound) bone-in turkey breast
2 tablespoons unsalted margarine, melted
½ teaspoon granulated garlic
¼ teaspoon poultry seasoning
⅛ teaspoon salt
⅛ teaspoon dried parsley

1. Preheat the air fryer to 350°F. Line the air fryer bushel with material and shower delicately with oil.
2. Place the turkey bosom in the pre-arranged bin, bosom side up, splash with oil, and cook for 20 minutes. Flip and cook, bosom side down, for an additional 20 minutes. Flip again and cook for an additional 15 minutes, until the inside temperature arrives at 165°F.
3. In a little bowl, combine as one the liquefied spread, garlic, poultry preparing, salt, and parsley.
4. Brush the margarine combination all around the turkey and cook for an additional 5 minutes, or until the skin is seared and crispy.

Fry Fact: Don't stress assuming that the turkey fits a little cozily in the bushel; it will recoil as it cooks. On the off chance that your fryer fits a 5-pound bosom, twofold the flavors prior to cooking. Cook for 32 minutes, flip, and cook for an additional 12 minutes. Flip again and cook for another 12 minutes, then brush with the butter mixture and cook for a final 5 minutes.

Per serving: Calories: 418; Total fat: 22g; Saturated fat: 8g; Cholesterol: 163mg; Sodium: 257mg; Carbohydrates: 0g; Fiber: 0g; Protein: 50g

CHAPTER 5
BEEF, PORK, AND LAMB

Meatball Subs Garlic
Butter Steak Bites Steak
Tips and Potatoes
Chicken-Fried Steak
Mongolian-Style Beef
Beef Jerky Blue
cheese Burgers Chinese-
Inspired Spareribs Bacon-
Wrapped Hot Dogs
Crescent Dogs Pork
Stuffing Meatballs
Sausage and Peppers
Honey-Garlic Pork Chops
Pork Schnitzel Pork Belly
Bites Honey Baked Ham
Brown Sugar and Mustard Ham
Steaks Ham and Cheese Pockets
Herbed Lamb Steaks Mustard
Lamb Chops

SAUSAGE AND PEPPERS

MEATBALL SUBS

FAMILY FAVORITE

Serves 6/Prep Time: 15 minutes/Fry Time: 19 minutes

Air-seared meatballs are stacked into a bun and canvassed in sauce and liquefied cheddar. Regardless of whether you make these subs for a weeknight dinner or a game-day nibble, they make certain to have everybody raving.

Oil, for spraying
1 pound 85% fit ground beef
½ cup Italian bread crumbs
1 tablespoon dried minced onion
1 tablespoon minced garlic
1 enormous egg
1 teaspoon salt
1 teaspoon newly ground dark pepper 6 hoagie rolls
1 (18-ounce) container marinara sauce
1½ cups destroyed mozzarella cheese

1. Line the air fryer bin with material and shower softly with oil.
2. In a huge bowl, combine as one the ground hamburger, bread morsels, onion, garlic, egg, salt, and dark pepper. Fold the combination into 18 meatballs.
3. Place the meatballs in the arranged basket.
4. Cook at 390°F for 15 minutes.
5. Place 3 meatballs in every hoagie roll. Top with marinara and mozzarella cheese.
6. Place the stacked rolls in the air fryer and cook for 3 to 4 minutes, or until the cheddar is softened. You might have to work in clumps, contingent upon the size of your air fryer. Serve immediately.

Faster Frying: Make this supper very speedy by cooking frozen meatballs at 350°F for 10 minutes. Or then again make the meatballs the other day and refrigerate them until prepared to cook.

Per serving: Calories: 434; Total fat: 21g; Saturated fat: 9g; Cholesterol: 105mg; Sodium: 810mg; Carbohydrates: 33g; Fiber: 3g; Protein: 28g

GARLIC BUTTER STEAK BITES

Serves 3/Prep Time: 5 minutes/Fry Time: 16 minutes

These delicate, delicious, reduced down bits of steak simply dissolve in your mouth. Ribeye, sirloin, or tri-tip are great slices to use here. This formula makes an extraordinary starter, or you can transform it into a speedy weeknight supper with a basic side dish. Add the extras to a serving of mixed greens or a pita pocket for lunch.

Oil, for spraying
1 pound boneless steak, cut into 1-inch pieces
2 tablespoons olive oil
1 teaspoon Worcestershire sauce
½ teaspoon granulated garlic
½ teaspoon salt
¼ teaspoon newly ground dark pepper

1. Preheat the air fryer to 400°F. Line the air fryer bushel with material and splash delicately with oil.
2. In a medium bowl, join the steak, olive oil, Worcestershire sauce, garlic, salt, and dark pepper and throw until equitably coated.
3. Place the steak in a solitary layer in the pre-arranged container. You might need to work in bunches, contingent upon the size of your air fryer.
4. Cook for 10 to 16 minutes, flipping each 3 to 4 minutes. The absolute cooking time will rely upon the thickness of the meat and your favored doneness. Assuming you need it cooked all the way through, it might take up to 5 extra minutes.

Pair It With: Broccoli-Cheddar Twice-Baked Potatoes or Bacon Potatoes and Green Beans would make a great accompaniment.

Per serving: Calories: 425; Total fat: 34g; Saturated fat: 12g; Cholesterol: 103mg; Sodium: 456mg; Carbohydrates: 1g; Fiber: 0g; Protein: 29g

STEAK TIPS AND POTATOES

FAMILY FAVORITE

Serves 4/Prep Time: 10 minutes/Fry Time: 20 minutes

Steak and potatoes are a definitive solace supper. Utilizing steak tips permits you to effortlessly control your parts. Use ribeye, sirloin, tri-tip, or hurl shoulder steaks.

Oil, for spraying
8 ounces child gold potatoes, cut in half
½ teaspoon salt
1 pound steak, cut into ½-inch pieces
1 teaspoon Worcestershire sauce
1 teaspoon granulated garlic
½ teaspoon salt
½ teaspoon newly ground dark pepper

1. Line the air fryer bin with material and splash gently with oil.
2. In a microwave-safe bowl, join the potatoes and salt, then, at that point, pour in about ½ inch of water. Microwave for 7 minutes, or until the potatoes are almost delicate. Drain.
3. In an enormous bowl, delicately combine as one the steak, potatoes, Worcestershire sauce, garlic, salt, and dark pepper. Spread the combination in an even layer in the arranged basket.
4. Cook at 400°F for 12 to 17 minutes, blending following 5 to 6 minutes. The cooking time will rely upon the thickness of the meat and favored doneness.

Change It Up: For a lower-carb feast, supplant the potatoes with mushrooms, asparagus, or zucchini.

Per serving: Calories: 303; Total fat: 19g; Saturated fat: 8g; Cholesterol: 77mg; Sodium: 674mg; Carbohydrates: 10g; Fiber: 1g; Protein: 23g

CAN YOU FRY IT?

CLASSIC STEAK

Line the air fryer basket with parchment and spray lightly with oil. Cook a 6-ounce steak at 400°F for 7 minutes, flipping after 4 minutes. This will produce a medium-rare steak. Adjust the time depending on your preferred doneness. Let rest for 10 minutes before cutting.

CHICKEN-FRIED STEAK

Serves 2/Prep Time: 20 minutes/Fry Time: 14 minutes

This breaded 3D square steak is generally covered in player and pan fried until brilliant. When presented with sauce and a side of pureed potatoes, it's the encapsulation of Southern solace food. This faultless adaptation has 90% less fat and oil.

FOR THE STEAK

Oil, for spraying
¾ cup generally useful
flour 1 teaspoon salt
1 teaspoon newly ground dark pepper
½ teaspoon paprika
½ teaspoon onion powder
1 teaspoon granulated garlic
¾ cup buttermilk
½ teaspoon hot sauce
2 (5-ounce) block steaks

FOR THE GRAVY

2 tablespoons unsalted spread 2
tablespoons universally handy
flour 1 cup milk
½ teaspoon salt
½ teaspoon newly ground dark pepper TO

MAKE THE STEAK

1. Line the air fryer crate with material and shower delicately with oil.
2. In a medium bowl, combine as one the flour, salt, dark pepper, paprika, onion powder, and garlic.
3. In another bowl, whisk together the buttermilk and hot sauce.
4. Dredge the steaks in the flour combination, plunge in the buttermilk blend, and dig again in the flour until totally covered. Shake off any overabundance flour.
5. Place the steaks in the pre-arranged bushel and splash generously with oil.
6. Cook at 400°F for 7 minutes, flip, shower with oil, and cook for one more 6 to 7 minutes, or until firm and browned.

TO MAKE THE GRAVY

7. In a little pot, whisk together the spread and flour over medium hotness until the margarine is dissolved. Gradually add the milk, salt, and dark pepper, increment the hotness to medium-high, and keep on cooking, blending continually, until the combination thickens. Eliminate from the heat.
8. Transfer the steaks to plates and pour the sauce over the top. Serve immediately.

Per serving: Calories: 641; Total fat: 28g; Saturated fat: 15g; Cholesterol: 151mg; Sodium: 1843mg; Carbohydrates: 53g; Fiber: 2g; Protein: 43g

MONGOLIAN-STYLE BEEF

FAMILY FAVORITE

Serves 4/Prep Time: 10 minutes/Fry Time: 10 minutes

Despite its name, this lasting takeout most loved began in Taiwan. Go ahead and trade out the meat with pork, chicken, or lamb.

Oil, for spraying
¼ cup cornstarch
1 pound flank steak, meagerly sliced
¾ cup stuffed light brown sugar
½ cup soy sauce
2 teaspoons toasted sesame oil
1 tablespoon minced garlic
½ teaspoon ground ginger
½ cup water
Cooked white rice or ramen noodles, for serving

1. Line the air fryer crate with material and shower softly with oil.
2. Place the cornstarch in a bowl and dig the steak until equitably covered. Shake off any abundance cornstarch.
3. Place the steak in the pre-arranged bin and shower daintily with oil.
4. Cook at 390°F for 5 minutes, flip, and cook for another 5 minutes.
5. In a little pot, join the earthy colored sugar, soy sauce, sesame oil, garlic, ginger, and water and heat to the point of boiling over medium-high hotness, blending much of the time. Eliminate from the heat.

6. Transfer the meat to the sauce and throw until equitably covered. Let sit for around 5 minutes so the steak retains the flavors. Present with white rice or ramen noodles.

Pair It With: Serve with Cream Cheese Wontons or Asiago Shishito Peppers.

Per serving: Calories: 509; Total fat: 9g; Saturated fat: 3g; Cholesterol: 68mg; Sodium: 1654mg; Carbohydrates: 77g; Fiber: 0g; Protein: 29g

BEEF JERKY

FAMILY FAVORITE

Serves 8/Prep Time: 5 minutes, in addition to 30 minutes to marinate/Fry Time: 2 hours

Homemade meat jerky preferences such a ton better than locally acquired and it has no additives! Take it with you while setting up camp or on travels, or simply appreciate as a midafternoon snack.

Oil, for spraying
1 pound round steak, cut into dainty, short slices
¼ cup soy sauce
3 tablespoons stuffed light earthy colored sugar 1 tablespoon minced garlic
1 teaspoon ground ginger
1 tablespoon water

1. Line the air fryer bin with material and shower softly with oil.
2. Place the steak, soy sauce, earthy colored sugar, garlic, ginger, and water in a zip-top plastic pack, seal, and shake well until equally covered. Refrigerate for 30 minutes.
3. Place the steak in the pre-arranged container in a solitary layer. You might have to work in bunches, contingent upon the size of your air fryer.
4. Cook at 180°F for no less than 2 hours. Add additional time assuming you like your jerky a piece tougher.

Change It Up: If you like hot jerky, add a couple of runs of your cherished hot sauce or season with vinegar and horseradish, Cajun preparing, garlic and dark pepper, or dry farm seasoning.

Per serving: Calories: 104; Total fat: 4g; Saturated fat: 1g; Cholesterol: 35mg; Sodium: 475mg; Carbohydrates: 4g; Fiber: 0g; Protein: 13g

BLUE CHEESE BURGERS

FAMILY FAVORITE

Serves 4/Prep Time: 10 minutes/Fry Time: 18 minutes

You can air fry burgers quicker than it takes to start up the barbecue, and the outcome is similarly as scrumptious, particularly when finished off with intense blue cheese.

Oil, for spraying
1 pound 90% lean ground beef
1 teaspoon Worcestershire sauce
½ teaspoon granulated garlic
½ teaspoon salt
¼ teaspoon newly ground dark pepper 1 tablespoon olive oil
8 tablespoons disintegrated blue cheddar, isolated 2 tablespoons bacon bits, divided
2 tablespoons grill sauce, separated 4 brioche buns

1. Line the air fryer crate with material and shower gently with oil.
2. In a huge bowl, combine as one the ground meat, Worcestershire sauce, garlic, salt, and dark pepper. Partition the combination into 4 pieces and structure them into patties.
3. Place the patties in the pre-arranged bin and brush with the olive oil. You might have to work in bunches, contingent upon the size of your air fryer.
4. Cook at 375°F for 7 to 8 minutes, flip, and cook for one more 7 to 8 minutes.
5. Top with the blue cheddar and bacon pieces and cook for one more 1 to 2 minutes, or until the cheddar is marginally melted.
6. Spread the grill sauce on the buns and top with the patties.

Change It Up: The prospects are unending with regards to burgers. Brush them with grill sauce and top with onion rings; go exemplary with lettuce, tomato, ketchup, and mustard; or zest things up with pepper Jack cheddar and cut jalapeños.

Per serving: Calories: 383; Total fat: 19g; Saturated fat: 6g; Cholesterol: 80mg; Sodium: 630mg; Carbohydrates: 23g; Fiber: 1g; Protein: 29g

CHINESE-INSPIRED SPARERIBS

FAMILY FAVORITE

Serves 4/Prep Time: 5 minutes, in addition to 30 minutes to marinate/Fry Time: 8 minutes

This simple air-seared interpretation of the exemplary dish utilizes boneless pork that has been cut into dainty strips and marinated in a heavenly sweet and exquisite sauce.

They're so quick to make, and the kind of the pork matches so well with steamed rice and vegetables, you could possibly need to make a twofold batch.

Oil, for spraying
12 ounces boneless pork spareribs, cut into 3-inch-long pieces
1 cup soy sauce
¾ cup sugar
½ cup meat or chicken stock
¼ cup honey
2 tablespoons minced garlic
1 teaspoon ground ginger
2 drops red food shading (optional)

1. Line the air fryer bushel with material and shower delicately with oil.
2. Combine the ribs, soy sauce, sugar, hamburger stock, honey, garlic, ginger, and food shading (if utilizing) in an enormous zip-top plastic sack, seal, and shake well until totally covered. Refrigerate for something like 30 minutes.
3. Place the ribs in the arranged basket.
4. Cook at 375°F for 8 minutes, or until the inward temperature arrives at 165°F.

Change It Up: You can likewise make this formula with boneless pork midsection or boneless pork chops.

Per serving: Calories: 199; Total fat: 5g; Saturated fat: 2g; Cholesterol: 63mg; Sodium: 837mg; Carbohydrates: 19g; Fiber: 0g; Protein: 19g

CAN YOU FRY IT?
BACON

Line the air fryer basket with parchment and spray lightly with oil. Place the bacon in a single layer in the prepared basket and cook at 400°F for 7 to 10 minutes, depending on the thickness of the bacon and your desired crispiness.

BACON-WRAPPED HOT DOGS

FAMILY FAVORITE
SUPER-FAST

Serves 4/Prep Time: 5 minutes/Fry Time: 10 minutes

Bacon-wrapped wieners are a staple among Southern California road sellers, who here and there call them Danger Dogs, Heart Attack Dogs, or Dirty Dogs. They're normally barbecued rather than steamed or bubbled, and you can utilize the air fryer to handily recreate their powerful taste and texture.

Oil, for splashing
4 bacon slices
4 all-hamburger franks
4 wiener buns
Toppings of choice

1. Line the air fryer bin with material and shower daintily with oil.
2. Wrap a piece of bacon firmly around each sausage, taking consideration to cover the tips so they don't get excessively fresh. Secure with a toothpick at each finish to keep the bacon from shrinking.
3. Place the franks in the arranged basket.
4. Cook at 380°F for 8 to 9 minutes, contingent upon how firm you like the bacon. For extra-fresh, cook the sausages at 400°F for 6 to 8 minutes.
5. Place the wieners in the buns, return them to the air fryer, and cook for one more 1 to 2 minutes, or until the buns are warm. Add your ideal garnishes and serve.

Change It Up: To make these bona fide Danger Dogs, top them with ketchup, mustard, mayonnaise, sautéed onions and chime peppers, and 1 entire green poblano chile.

Per serving: Calories: 329; Total fat: 20g; Saturated fat: 7g; Cholesterol: 39mg; Sodium: 900mg; Carbohydrates: 23g; Fiber: 1g; Protein: 13g

CRESCENT DOGS

FAMILY FAVORITE

Makes 24 bow canines/Prep Time: 15 minutes/Fry Time: 8 minutes

Often called pigs in a cover, these reduced down frankfurters enveloped by sickle roll mixture are incredible for parties. On the off chance that you have goofs off, they'll cherish assisting with the prep.

Oil, for spraying
1 (8-ounce) can refrigerated sickle rolls 8
cuts cheddar, cut into thirds
24 mixed drink hotdogs or 8 (6-inch) franks, cut into
thirds 2 tablespoons unsalted spread, melted
1 tablespoon ocean salt flakes

1. Line the air fryer crate with material and shower daintily with oil.
2. Separate the batter into 8 triangles. Cut every triangle into 3 tight triangles so you have 24 complete triangles.
3. Top every triangle with 1 piece of cheddar and 1 mixed drink sausage.
4. Roll up each piece of mixture, beginning at the wide end and moving toward the point.
5. Place the rolls in the pre-arranged bushel in a solitary layer. You might have to cook in groups, contingent upon the size of your air fryer.
6. Cook at 325°F for 3 to 4 minutes, flip, and cook for one more 3 to 4 minutes, or until brilliant brown.
7. Brush with the liquefied margarine and sprinkle with the ocean salt chips before serving.

Change It Up: Brush the wieners with grill sauce prior to moving in the mixture and baking. Serve chili cheese dip on the side for dipping. Or on the other hand make them into pretzel canines by utilizing the batter from Soft Pretzel Bites.

Per serving (2 sickle canines): Calories: 112; Total fat: 8g; Saturated fat: 4g; Cholesterol: 26mg; Sodium: 398mg; Carbohydrates: 5g; Fiber: 0g; Protein: 5g

PORK STUFFING MEATBALLS

FAMILY FAVORITE

Makes 35 meatballs/Prep Time: 10 minutes/Fry Time: 12 minutes

Meatballs make great hors d'oeuvres or party tidbits, and you can enhance them in such countless ways. This air-singed adaptation is less

fatty than customary meatballs.

Oil, for spraying
1½ pounds ground pork
1 cup bread crumbs
½ cup milk
¼ cup minced onion
1 enormous egg
1 tablespoon dried rosemary
1 tablespoon dried thyme
1 teaspoon salt
1 teaspoon newly ground dark pepper 1
teaspoon finely hacked new parsley

1. Line the air fryer bushel with material and splash gently with oil.
2. In a huge bowl, combine as one the ground pork, bread pieces, milk, onion, egg, rosemary, thyme, salt, dark pepper, and parsley.
3. Roll around 2 tablespoons of the combination into a ball. Rehash with the remainder of the blend. You ought to have 30 to 35 meatballs.
4. Place the meatballs in the pre-arranged bushel in a solitary layer, leaving space between every one. You might have to work in clumps, contingent upon the size of your air fryer.
5. Cook at 390°F for 10 to 12 minutes, flipping following 5 minutes, or until brilliant brown and the interior temperature arrives at 160°F.

Change It Up: Serve the meatballs with spaghetti and marinara for an exemplary supper combo, or throw with grill sauce and jam or with prepared sauce. Serve them in a hoagie, over rice, or with sauce and crushed potatoes.

Per serving (5 meatballs): Calories: 342; Total fat: 22g; Saturated fat: 8g; Cholesterol: 98mg; Sodium: 518mg; Carbohydrates: 13g; Fiber: 1g; Protein: 20g

SAUSAGE AND PEPPERS

FAMILY FAVORITE
GLUTEN-FREE

Serves 4/Prep Time: 7 minutes/Fry Time: 35 minutes

A conventional Italian-American dish frequently found at road fairs and amusement parks, hotdog and peppers can stand its ground as a full supper, in spite of the fact that it's additionally incredible thrown in pasta with

pureed tomatoes or stuffed into a sandwich.

Oil, for spraying
2 pounds hot or sweet Italian frankfurter joins, cut into thick cuts 4 enormous ringer peppers of any tone, cultivated and cut into slices
1 onion, daintily cut
1 tablespoon olive oil
1 tablespoon cleaved new parsley 1 teaspoon dried oregano
1 teaspoon dried basil
1 teaspoon balsamic vinegar

1. Line the air fryer crate with material and splash gently with oil.
2. In a huge bowl, consolidate the wiener, chime peppers, and onion.
3. In a little bowl, whisk together the olive oil, parsley, oregano, basil, and balsamic vinegar. Pour the blend over the wiener and peppers and throw until uniformly coated.
4. Using an opened spoon, move the combination to the pre-arranged bin, taking consideration to deplete out as much overabundance fluid as possible.
5. Cook at 350°F for 20 minutes, mix, and cook for an additional 15 minutes, or until the hotdog is carmelized and the juices run clear.

Change It Up: Combine this dish with cooked white rice and taco preparing or enchilada sauce; utilize the chiles of your decision rather than ringer peppers; or use asparagus, green beans, or zucchini rather than onions and chime peppers.

Per serving: Calories: 428; Total fat: 23g; Saturated fat: 8g; Cholesterol: 68mg; Sodium: 943mg; Carbohydrates: 17g; Fiber: 4g; Protein: 39g

HONEY-GARLIC PORK CHOPS

FAMILY FAVORITE
GLUTEN-FREE

Serves 4/Prep Time: 5 minutes/Fry Time: 15 minutes

A coating made with honey, garlic, lemon juice, and sweet stew sauce gives these pork cleaves the ideal smidgen of pleasantness in each bite.

Oil, for spraying

4 (6-ounce) boneless pork hacks
1 teaspoon salt
½ teaspoon newly ground dark pepper
¼ cup honey
2 tablespoons minced garlic
2 tablespoons lemon juice
1 tablespoon sweet stew sauce

1. Line the air fryer container with material and shower gently with oil. Season the two sides of the pork hacks with the salt and dark pepper.
2. Place the cleaves in a solitary layer in the pre-arranged crate. You might have to work in clusters, contingent upon the size of your air fryer.
3. Cook at 400°F for 8 minutes, flip, and cook for an additional 7 minutes, or until the inside temperature arrives at 145°F.
4. In a little pan, consolidate the honey, garlic, lemon juice, and sweet stew sauce and bring to a stew over low hotness. Cook until the sauce thickens, 3 to 4 minutes. It will thicken considerably more as it cools.
5. Transfer the hacks to a serving platter and pour the sauce over the top.

Change It Up: Try the cleaves covered in simmered ringer peppers, covered in fresh panko, showered with mushroom sauce or French onion sauce, or brushed with grill sauce. You can add two or three hints of hot sauce to the sauce blend on the off chance that you need somewhat added heat.

Per serving: Calories: 341; Total fat: 12g; Saturated fat: 4g; Cholesterol: 114mg; Sodium: 722mg; Carbohydrates: 20g; Fiber: 0g; Protein: 37g

PORK SCHNITZEL

FAMILY FAVORITE

Serves 4/Prep Time: 10 minutes/Fry Time: 14 minutes

Wiener schnitzel is a veal cutlet covered in bread morsels and seared. This sound option is made with lean pork chops.

Oil, for spraying
⅔ cup panko bread crumbs
¼ teaspoon granulated garlic
¼ teaspoon dried thyme
¼ teaspoon dried sage
¼ teaspoon dried rosemary

¼ teaspoon salt
¼ teaspoon newly ground dark pepper
½ cup universally handy flour
1 enormous egg
4 boneless pork slashes, beat to ⅓ inch thick

1. Preheat the air fryer to 390°F. Line the air fryer bushel with material and shower daintily with oil.
2. In a medium bowl, combine as one the bread scraps, garlic, thyme, sage, rosemary, salt, and dark pepper.
3. Place the flour on a plate.
4. In a little bowl, whisk the egg.
5. Dredge the cleaves in the flour, dunk in the egg, and dig in the bread piece blend until equitably coated.
6. Place the hacks in a solitary layer in the pre-arranged bin and splash with oil. You might have to work in groups, contingent upon the size of your air fryer.
7. Cook for 8 minutes, flip, splash with oil, and cook for one more 5 to 6 minutes, or until brilliant brown and the inward temperature arrives at 145°F.

Pair It With: Serve with Garlic-Parmesan Crispy Baby Potatoes on the side and Shortbread Cookie Sticks for dessert.

Per serving: Calories: 340; Total fat: 13g; Saturated fat: 4g; Cholesterol: 141mg; Sodium: 297mg; Carbohydrates: 18g; Fiber: 1g; Protein: 35g

PORK BELLY BITES

FAMILY FAVORITE

Serves 4/Prep Time: 10 minutes/Fry Time: 18 minutes

If you desire soften in-your-mouth pork gut, get ready to become fixated on this formula. It's delicious and delightful, and consistently makes you want more of more.

Oil, for spraying
1 pound pork stomach, cleaned and cut into 1-inch blocks
2 teaspoons Worcestershire sauce
1 teaspoon soy sauce

1 teaspoon granulated garlic
¼ teaspoon salt
¼ teaspoon newly ground dark pepper
⅓ cup grill sauce

1. Line the air fryer crate with material and splash softly with oil.
2. In a medium bowl, combine as one the pork, Worcestershire sauce, soy sauce, garlic, salt, and dark pepper.
3. Place the pork in a solitary layer in the pre-arranged bushel. You might have to work in clusters, contingent upon the size of your air fryer.
4. Cook at 400°F for 12 to 18 minutes, flipping each 3 to 4 minutes. The real cooking time will rely upon the thickness of the pork and your favored doneness. It ought to be delicate yet the juices ought to be clear or just marginally pink.
5. Transfer to a bowl and prepare with the grill sauce before serving.

Change It Up: While I like to partake in this dish all alone as a starter, you can likewise serve it in a bun or a pita, blend it into macaroni and cheddar, or add it to a plate of mixed greens. For an alternate flavor, take a stab at preparing with salad dressing or your beloved Asian sauce.

Per serving: Calories: 631; Total fat: 60g; Saturated fat: 21g; Cholesterol: 82mg; Sodium: 475mg; Carbohydrates: 10g; Fiber: 0g; Protein: 11g

HONEY BAKED HAM

FAMILY FAVORITE
GLUTEN-FREE

Serves 12/Prep Time: 7 minutes/Fry Time: 35 minutes

You don't need to consign ham to Sunday supper or save it for these special seasons; get a precooked ham at the supermarket and use your air fryer to get this exquisite sweet dinner on the table in under an hour.

Oil, for spraying
½ cup stuffed light earthy colored sugar 2 tablespoons pineapple juice
2 tablespoons apple juice vinegar
1 tablespoon honey
1 teaspoon paprika
1 teaspoon cayenne pepper

¼ teaspoon ground cinnamon
¼ teaspoon ground nutmeg
¼ teaspoon salt
1 (2-to 3-pound) completely cooked cut boneless smoked ham

1. Line the air fryer bushel with material and splash daintily with oil.
2. In a little bowl, whisk together the earthy colored sugar, pineapple juice, apple juice vinegar, honey, paprika, cayenne pepper, cinnamon, nutmeg, and salt.
3. Place the ham on an enormous piece of aluminum foil and pour one-fourth of the coating over the top. Crease the foil around the ham to shut it down and cover it completely.
4. Place the enveloped ham by the arranged basket.
5. Cook at 320°F for 15 minutes. Open the foil, sprinkle the ham with more coating, close the foil, and cook for an additional 10 minutes. Open once again, add more coating, close the foil, and cook for an additional 10 minutes, or until the inward temperature arrives at 140°F. The genuine cooking time will shift contingent upon the size of the ham.
6. Transfer the ham to a serving plate and pour any excess coating over the top.

Change It Up: Change up the coating by adding ¼ cup whiskey, 1 or 2 tablespoons mustard, 1 tablespoon stew sauce, 3 tablespoons earthy colored spread, ¼ cup cola, or 1 or 2 tablespoons molasses.

Per serving: Calories: 167; Total fat: 4g; Saturated fat: 1g; Cholesterol: 65mg; Sodium: 1066mg; Carbohydrates: 12g; Fiber: 0g; Protein: 22g

BROWN SUGAR AND MUSTARD HAM STEAKS

GLUTEN-FREE
SUPER-FAST

Serves 2/Prep Time: 2 minutes/Fry Time: 12 minutes

This formula makes a generous breakfast with a side of eggs over simple, or a delectable supper with sauce and home fries. The fixings impeccably caramelize in the air fryer, and any wreck is kept to a minimum.

Oil, for spraying
2 tablespoons unsalted margarine, melted
2 tablespoons pressed light earthy
colored sugar 1 teaspoon honey
1 teaspoon mustard
1 (3-ounce) ham steak

1. Preheat the air fryer to 380°F. Line the air fryer bin with material and splash softly with oil.
2. In a little bowl, whisk together the margarine, earthy colored sugar, honey, and mustard.
3. Place the ham steak in the pre-arranged container and shower half of the spread blend over the top.
4. Cook for 5 to 6 minutes, flip, add the excess spread sauce, and cook for one more 5 to 6 minutes, until warmed through.
5. Cut the ham steak fifty-fifty and serve.

Change It Up: You can make this recipe using leftovers from the Honey Baked Ham. Try cutting it in slices and adding them to a sandwich for lunch with some egg salad or Hard-Boiled Eggs on the side.

Per serving: Calories: 192; Total fat: 13g; Saturated fat: 8g; Cholesterol: 48mg; Sodium: 566mg; Carbohydrates: 12g; Fiber: 0g; Protein: 7g

HAM AND CHEESE POCKETS

FAMILY FAVORITE

Serves 4/Prep Time: 10 minutes/Fry Time: 12 minutes

A definitive handheld solace food, natively constructed ham and cheddar pockets are firm outwardly and delicate within. With a low-fat outside layer, they are such a ton better (and better for you) than the locally acquired frozen ones. Attempt them as a fast and simple hot breakfast.

Oil, for spraying
2 cups self-rising flour, in addition to
additional for tidying 2 cups plain Greek
yogurt
4 cuts store ham
4 cuts cheddar 1 huge
egg
1 teaspoon water

1. Line the air fryer bin with material and shower daintily with oil.
2. In a huge bowl, combine as one the flour and yogurt until it frames a mixture. The mixture can be tacky, so flour your hands as needed.
3. Roll out the batter to ¼ inch thick and cut it into 8 (4-by-5-inch) square shapes. You might have to reroll the pieces of batter to get 8 rectangles.
4. Top 4 square shapes with the ham and cheddar cuts. Cover with the excess square shapes and press around the edges to seal.
5. In a little bowl, beat the egg and water together. Brush the two sides of the mixture with the egg wash.
6. Place the pockets in the pre-arranged crate and splash with oil.
7. Cook at 370°F for 9 minutes, flip, shower with oil once more, and cook for an additional 3 minutes, or until brilliant brown.

Faster Frying: Speed up the planning time by utilizing refrigerated bow roll batter as opposed to making and moving custom made mixture. Cook for 10 minutes, flipping midway through.

Per serving: Calories: 456; Total fat: 17g; Saturated fat: 9g; Cholesterol: 100mg; Sodium: 994mg; Carbohydrates: 52g; Fiber: 2g; Protein: 23g

HERBED LAMB STEAKS

FAMILY FAVORITE
GLUTEN-FREE

Serves 4/Prep Time: 10 minutes, in addition to 30 minutes to marinate/Fry Time: 15 minutes

Roasting an entire leg of sheep is a not kidding responsibility, yet on the off chance that you are longing for this heavenly lean meat, attempt air broiling sheep steaks. They will concoct rapidly and reliably, and you'll partake in all the flavor with no of the fuss.

½ medium onion
2 tablespoons minced garlic
2 teaspoons ground ginger
1 teaspoon ground cinnamon
1 teaspoon onion powder
1 teaspoon cayenne pepper
1 teaspoon salt
4 (6-ounce) boneless sheep sirloin steaks

Oil, for spraying

1. In a blender, consolidate the onion, garlic, ginger, cinnamon, onion powder, cayenne pepper, and salt and heartbeat until the onion is minced.
2. Place the sheep steaks in an enormous bowl or zip-top plastic sack and sprinkle the onion combination over the top. Turn the steaks until they are equitably covered. Cover with saran wrap or seal the pack and refrigerate for 30 minutes.
3. Preheat the air fryer to 330°F. Line the air fryer bin with material and splash softly with oil.
4. Place the sheep steaks in a solitary layer in the pre-arranged bushel, ensuring they don't cover. You might have to work in bunches, contingent upon the size of your air fryer.
5. Cook for 8 minutes, flip, and cook for an additional 7 minutes, or until the inward temperature arrives at 155°F.

Faster Frying: Skip the onion marinade and season just with salt, newly ground dark pepper, and a sprinkle of onion powder, or utilize a packaged marinade or coating that requirements to sit for just a brief time before cooking.

Per serving: Calories: 368; Total fat: 24g; Saturated fat: 12g; Cholesterol: 112mg; Sodium: 683mg; Carbohydrates: 3g; Fiber: 1g; Protein: 32g

MUSTARD LAMB CHOPS

FAMILY FAVORITE
GLUTEN-FREE

Serves 4/Prep Time: 5 minutes/Fry Time: 14 minutes

Lamb hacks make a happy dinner when you're facilitating visitors or commending a unique event. Sheep will in general have less marbleizing than different meats, so it's much more streamlined, however it has a lot of flavor.

Oil, for spraying
1 tablespoon Dijon mustard
2 teaspoons lemon juice
½ teaspoon dried tarragon
¼ teaspoon salt
¼ teaspoon newly ground dark pepper 4
(1¼-inch-thick) flank sheep chops

1. Preheat the air fryer to 390°F. Line the air fryer bushel with material and splash softly with oil.
2. In a little bowl, combine as one the mustard, lemon juice, tarragon, salt, and dark pepper.
3. Pat dry the sheep slashes with a paper towel. Brush the slashes on the two sides with the mustard mixture.
4. Place the cleaves in the pre-arranged container. You might have to work in groups, contingent upon the size of your air fryer.
5. Cook for 8 minutes, flip, and cook for an additional 6 minutes, or until the inward temperature arrives at 125°F for uncommon, 145°F for medium-uncommon, or 155°F for medium.

Pair It With: Serve with Crispy Butternut Squash or Everything Bagel Brussels Sprouts.

Per serving: Calories: 341; Total fat: 29g; Saturated fat: 13g; Cholesterol: 78mg; Sodium: 260mg; Carbohydrates: 1g; Fiber: 0g; Protein: 18g

CHAPTER 8
DESSERTS

Fried Cream-Filled Sponge Cakes
Fried Cream-Filled Sandwich Cookies
Elephant Ears
S'mores
Beignets
Funnel Cake
Churro Bites
Apple Fries
Apple Pie Egg Rolls
Grilled Peaches Blueberry
Hand Pies Berry
Cheesecake Meringue
Cookies Shortbread Cookie
Sticks Chocolate-Stuffed
Wontons Chocolate Lava
Cakes Overload Dessert
Pizza Chocolate Mug
Cakes

BLUEBERRY HAND PIES

FRIED CREAM-FILLED SPONGE

CAKES

FAMILY FAVORITE
VEGETARIAN

Makes 4 cakes/Prep Time: 10 minutes/Fry Time: 10 minutes

Deep-seared cream-filled wipe cakes are an absurd amusement park treat. This lighter variant holds all the notable flavor with simply a small portion of the calories and fat.

Oil, for spraying
1 (8-ounce) can refrigerated bow rolls 4
cream-filled wipe cakes
1 tablespoon confectioners' sugar

1. Line the air fryer container with material and shower delicately with oil.
2. Unroll the mixture into a solitary level layer and cut it into 4 equivalent pieces.
3. Place 1 wipe cake in the focal point of each piece of batter. Fold the batter over the cake, squeezing the closures to seal.
4. Place the enveloped cakes by the pre-arranged crate and splash delicately with oil.
5. Cook at 200°F for 5 minutes, flip, shower with oil, and cook for an additional 5 minutes, or until brilliant brown.
6. Dust with the confectioners' sugar and serve.

Change It Up: You can make this formula utilizing other cream-filled cakes or cakes, or serve it with a plunging sauce of chocolate or organic product syrup on the side.

Per serving (1 cake): Calories: 349; Total fat: 12g; Saturated fat: 3g; Cholesterol: 18mg; Sodium: 579mg; Carbohydrates: 55g; Fiber: 1g; Protein: 5g

FRIED CREAM-FILLED SANDWICH COOKIES

FAMILY FAVORITE
VEGETARIAN

Makes 8 treats/Prep Time: 8 minutes/Fry Time: 8 minutes

The cream-filled sandwich treat has been a dearest top pick for over 100 years. This air-singed take will make everybody swoon.

Oil, for spraying
1 (8-ounce) can refrigerated sickle rolls
¼ cup milk
8 cream-filled sandwich treats 1 tablespoon confectioners' sugar

1. Line the air fryer bin with material and splash softly with oil.
2. Unroll the bow batter and separate it into 8 triangles. Spread out the triangles on a work surface.
3. Pour the milk into a shallow bowl. Straightaway dunk every treat in the milk, then, at that point, place in the focal point of a batter triangle.
4. Wrap the mixture around the treat, removing any overabundance and squeezing the finishes to seal. You might have the option to consolidate the abundance into enough mixture to cover extra treats, if desired.
5. Place the enclosed treats by the pre-arranged bin, crease side down, and shower delicately with oil.
6. Cook at 350°F for 4 minutes, flip, splash with oil, and cook for one more 3 to 4 minutes, or until puffed and brilliant brown.
7. Dust with the confectioners' sugar and serve.

Change It Up: Try this formula utilizing your beloved peanut butter sandwich treat or cereal cream pie treat. Assuming the treats are delicate, you don't need to dunk them in milk.

Per serving (1 treat): Calories: 149; Total fat: 6g; Saturated fat: 1g; Cholesterol: 1mg; Sodium: 315mg; Carbohydrates: 22g; Fiber: 0g; Protein: 3g

ELEPHANT EARS

FAMILY FAVORITE
SUPER-FAST
VEGETARIAN

Serves 8/Prep Time: 5 minutes/Fry Time: 5 minutes

Like their namesake creature, elephant ears are a larger than usual

enjoyment. They're generally presented with a shower of molasses, maple syrup, or corn syrup, however I like to tidy them with confectioners' sugar or top with a scoop of ice cream.

Oil, for spraying
1 (8-ounce) can buttermilk rolls 3 tablespoons sugar
1 tablespoon ground cinnamon
3 tablespoons unsalted margarine, liquefied 8 scoops vanilla frozen yogurt (optional)

1. Line the air fryer container with material and splash gently with oil.
2. Separate the mixture. Utilizing a moving pin, carry out the bread rolls into 6-to 8-inch circles.
3. Place the batter circles in the pre-arranged crate and splash generously with oil. You might have to work in groups, contingent upon the size of your air fryer.
4. Cook at 350°F for 5 minutes, or until delicately browned.
5. In a little bowl, combine as one the sugar and cinnamon.
6. Brush the elephant ears with the dissolved spread and sprinkle with the cinnamon-sugar mixture.
7. Top each presenting with a scoop of frozen yogurt (if using).

Change It Up: To make zeppole (Italian doughnuts), cut the batter into more modest pieces, cook for 3 minutes, shake, and cook for an additional 3 minutes. Cover with confectioners' sugar before serving.

Per serving: Calories: 151; Total fat: 8g; Saturated fat: 4g; Cholesterol: 12mg; Sodium: 311mg; Carbohydrates: 19g; Fiber: 1g; Protein: 2g

S'MORES

FAMILY FAVORITE
SUPER-FAST

Makes 8 s'mores/Prep Time: 5 minutes/Fry Time: 30 seconds

You needn't bother with an open air fire to appreciate s'mores. Truth be told, you don't need to be outside! The air fryer makes it simple to appreciate them any season of year.

Oil, for spraying
8 graham saltine squares 2
(1½-ounce) chocolate bars 4
enormous marshmallows

1. Line the air fryer bin with material and shower softly with oil.
2. Place 4 graham wafer squares in the arranged basket.
3. Break the chocolate bars into equal parts and spot 1 piece on top of every graham wafer. Top with 1 marshmallow.
4. Cook at 370°F for 30 seconds, or until the marshmallows are puffed and brilliant brown and somewhat melted.
5. Top with the excess graham saltine squares and serve.

Change It Up: Replace the chocolate bars with cut strawberries and chocolate-hazelnut spread, cut apples and caramel sauce, or peanut butter cups to differ the kinds of this classic.

Per serving (2 s'mores): Calories: 280; Total fat: 6g; Saturated fat: 3g; Cholesterol: 0mg; Sodium: 74mg; Carbohydrates: 19g; Fiber: 2g; Protein: 2g

BEIGNETS

FAMILY FAVORITE
VEGETARIAN

Makes 9 beignets/Prep Time: 15 minutes, in addition to 1 hour 30 minutes to rise/Fry Time: 6 minutes

These little glossed over pads are a New Orleans staple. Customarily the batter is seared like a doughnut, however this eased up adaptation has 90% less fat and is a virtuous pleasure.

Oil, for lubing and spraying
3 cups generally useful flour, in addition to additional for tidying 1½ teaspoons salt
1 (2¼-teaspoon) envelope dynamic dry yeast 1 cup milk
2 tablespoons pressed light earthy colored sugar 1 tablespoon unsalted butter
1 huge egg
1 cup confectioners' sugar

1. Oil a huge bowl.
2. In a little bowl, combine as one the flour, salt, and yeast. Set aside.
3. Pour the milk into a glass estimating cup and microwave in 1-minute stretches until it boils.
4. In an enormous bowl, combine as one the earthy colored sugar and margarine. Pour in the hot milk and rush until the sugar has broken up. Let cool to room temperature.
5. Whisk the egg into the cooled milk combination and overlap in the flour blend until a mixture forms.
6. On a softly floured work surface, ply the batter for 3 to 5 minutes.
7. Place the batter in the oiled bowl and cover with a perfect kitchen towel. Give rise access a warm spot for around 60 minutes, or until multiplied in size.
8. Roll the batter out on a gently floured work surface until it's about ¼ inch thick. Cut the mixture into 3-inch squares and spot them on a lightly
    floured baking sheet. Cover freely with a kitchen towel and let rise again until multiplied in size, around 30 minutes.
9. Line the air fryer container with material and shower delicately with oil.
10. Place the mixture squares in the pre-arranged crate and splash gently with oil. You might have to work in clumps, contingent upon the size of your air fryer.

11. Cook at 390°F for 3 minutes, flip, splash with oil, and cook for an additional 3 minutes, until crispy.
12. Dust with the confectioners' sugar before serving.

Faster Frying: To make this formula in under 10 minutes, utilize refrigerated bow batter cut into squares or triangles. Cook at 320°F for 6 minutes, flipping partially through, until crispy.

Per serving (1 beignet): Calories: 245; Total fat: 4g; Saturated fat: 2g; Cholesterol: 47mg; Sodium: 419mg; Carbohydrates: 46g; Fiber: 1g; Protein: 6g

FUNNEL CAKE

FAMILY FAVORITE
SUPER-FAST
VEGETARIAN

Serves 4/Prep Time: 10 minutes/Fry Time: 5 minutes

Funnel cake, which began in Pennsylvania Dutch nation, is one of the primary known singed food varieties in North America. This rendition is lighter, however it will in any case cause you to feel like you had a day at the fair.

Oil, for spraying
1 cup self-rising flour, in addition to
additional for tidying 1 cup sans fat vanilla
Greek yogurt
½ teaspoon ground cinnamon
¼ cup confectioners' sugar

1. Preheat the air fryer to 375°F. Line the air fryer container with material and shower softly with oil.
2. In a huge bowl, combine as one the flour, yogurt, and cinnamon until the combination shapes a ball.
3. Place the mixture on a gently floured work surface and massage for around 2 minutes.
4. Cut the batter into 4 equivalent pieces, then, at that point, cut every one of those into 6 pieces. You ought to have 24 complete pieces.
5. Roll the pieces into 8-to 10-inch-long ropes. Freely hill the ropes into 4 heaps of 6 ropes.
6. Place the batter heaps in the pre-arranged crate and splash generously

with oil. You might have to work in groups, contingent upon the size of your air fryer.
7. Cook for 5 minutes, or until softly browned.
8. Dust with the confectioners' sugar before serving.

Change It Up: While the exemplary adaptation is presented with just a tidying of confectioners' sugar, you can go over the top and add pie filling and whipped cream, shower with chocolate or caramel syrup, or
sprinkle with cinnamon-sugar and cream cheddar icing.

Per serving: Calories: 193; Total fat: 2g; Saturated fat: 1g; Cholesterol: 3mg; Sodium: 413mg; Carbohydrates: 38g; Fiber: 1g; Protein: 6g

CHURRO BITES

FAMILY FAVORITE
SUPER-FAST
VEGETARIAN

Makes 36 nibbles/Prep Time: 5 minutes/Fry Time: 6 minutes

Churros are habitually delighted in at amusement parks or as road food, yet you can make them at home at whatever point you get the craving.

Oil, for spraying
1 (17¼-ounce) bundle frozen puffed baked good,
defrosted 1 cup granulated sugar
1 tablespoon ground cinnamon
½ cup confectioners' sugar
1 tablespoon milk

1. Preheat the air fryer to 400°F. Line the air fryer container with material and shower delicately with oil.
2. Unfold the puff cake onto a spotless work surface. Utilizing a sharp blade, cut the batter into 36 reduced down pieces.
3. Place the mixture pieces in a single layer in the pre-arranged bushel, taking consideration not to allow the parts of touch or overlap.
4. Cook for 3 minutes, flip, and cook for an additional 3 minutes, or until puffed and golden.
5. In a little bowl, combine as one the granulated sugar and cinnamon.
6. In another little bowl, whisk together the confectioners' sugar and milk.

7. Dredge the chomps in the cinnamon-sugar combination until uniformly coated.
8. Serve with the what tops off an already good thing for dipping.

Change It Up: You can cut the puff cake mixture into long strips rather than nibbles, whenever wanted. The churros are likewise scrumptious when plunged in chocolate, caramel, or natural product syrup.

Per serving (3 chomps): Calories: 308; Total fat: 16g; Saturated fat: 4g; Cholesterol: 0mg; Sodium: 102mg; Carbohydrates: 40g; Fiber: 1g; Protein: 3g

APPLE FRIES

FAMILY FAVORITE
VEGETARIAN

Serves 8/Prep Time: 10 minutes/Fry Time: 7 minutes

If you love visiting apple plantations, this formula gives you the taste you revere in reduced down fries that make the ideal sweet or snack.

Oil, for spraying
1 cup universally handy flour
3 enormous eggs, beaten
1 cup graham wafer crumbs
¼ cup sugar
1 teaspoon ground cinnamon
3 huge Gala apples, stripped, cored, and cut into wedges
1 cup caramel sauce, warmed

1. Preheat the air fryer to 380°F. Line the air fryer bin with material and shower daintily with oil.
2. Place the flour and beaten eggs in discrete dishes and put away. In another bowl, combine as one the graham saltine morsels, sugar, and cinnamon.
3. Working each in turn, coat the apple wedges in the flour, dunk in the egg, and dig in the graham wafer blend until uniformly coated.
4. Place the apples in the pre-arranged container, taking consideration not to cover, and splash daintily with oil. You might have to work in bunches, contingent upon the size of your air fryer.
5. Cook for 5 minutes, flip, splash with oil, and cook for an additional 2

minutes, or until crunchy and brilliant brown.

6. Drizzle the caramel sauce over the top and serve.

Faster Frying: To save time on cutting, get a pack of presliced apples.

Per serving: Calories: 259; Total fat: 4g; Saturated fat: 1g; Cholesterol: 70mg; Sodium: 174mg; Carbohydrates: 53g; Fiber: 2g; Protein: 5g

APPLE PIE EGG ROLLS

FAMILY FAVORITE
VEGETARIAN

Makes 6 rolls/Prep Time: 10 minutes/Fry Time: 8 minutes

If you love fruity dessert filling, delay until you taste it inside a firm, crunchy egg roll covering. This formula is so much faster than making a standard pie, and better for you, too.

Oil, for spraying
1 (21-ounce) can fruity dessert
filling 1 tablespoon generally
useful flour
½ teaspoon lemon juice
¼ teaspoon ground nutmeg
¼ teaspoon ground cinnamon
6 egg roll wrappers

1. Preheat the air fryer to 400°F. Line the air fryer container with material and splash softly with oil.
2. In a medium bowl, combine as one the pie filling, flour, lemon juice, nutmeg, and cinnamon.
3. Lay out the egg roll coverings on a work surface and spoon a spot of pie filling in the focal point of each.
4. Fill a little bowl with water. Plunge your finger in the water and, working each in turn, saturate the edges of the coverings. Crease the covering like an envelope: First overlay one corner into the middle. Crease each side corner in, and afterward overlay over the leftover corner, ensuring each corner covers a little and the soaked edges stay shut. Utilize extra water and your fingers to seal any open edges.
5. Place the rolls in the pre-arranged container and shower generously

with oil. You might have to work in clumps, contingent upon the size of your air fryer.

6. Cook for 4 minutes, flip, splash with oil, and cook for an additional 4 minutes, or until firm and brilliant brown. Serve immediately.

Change It Up: Make these rolls with any flavor pie filling. Appreciate in a hurry or put them in a bowl and top with whipped cream or frozen yogurt and a sprinkle of nutmeg.

Per serving (1 roll): Calories: 205; Total fat: 1g; Saturated fat: 0g; Cholesterol: 3mg; Sodium: 230mg; Carbohydrates: 46g; Fiber: 2g; Protein: 3g

GRILLED PEACHES

FAMILY FAVORITE
SUPER-FAST
VEGETARIAN

Serves 4/Prep Time: 5 minutes/Fry Time: 10 minutes

As soon as the eighteenth century, peach trees were pretty much as bountiful as weeds across the southern United States. Subsequently, peach plans turned into an American custom. Finished off with a scoop of reviving vanilla frozen yogurt, these barbecued peaches are the ideal summer dessert.

Oil, for spraying
¼ cup graham wafer crumbs
¼ cup pressed light brown sugar
8 tablespoons (1 stick) unsalted spread, cubed
¼ teaspoon cinnamon
2 peaches, hollowed and cut into
quarters 4 scoops vanilla ice cream

1. Line the air fryer crate with material and splash daintily with oil.
2. In a little bowl, combine as one the graham saltine pieces, earthy colored sugar, margarine, and cinnamon with a fork until crumbly.
3. Place the peach wedges in the pre-arranged bushel, skin-side up. You might have to work in clusters, contingent upon the size of your air fryer.
4. Cook at 350°F for 5 minutes, flip, and sprinkle with a spoonful of the graham wafer blend. Cook for an additional 5 minutes, or until delicate and caramelized.

5. Top with a scoop of vanilla frozen yogurt and any excess disintegrate blend. Serve immediately.

Change It Up: Nectarines are a great swap for peaches. For a lighter adaptation, avoid the disintegrate combination and shower with honey before serving.

Per serving: Calories: 445; Total fat: 31g; Saturated fat: 19g; Cholesterol: 90mg; Sodium: 263mg; Carbohydrates: 40g; Fiber: 2g; Protein: 4g

BLUEBERRY HAND PIES

FAMILY FAVORITE
VEGETARIAN

Makes 12 pies/Prep Time: 15 minutes/Fry Time: 10 minutes

Baking a pie isn't known for being speedy or basic, however the air fryer makes it simple to prepare these basic hand pies in under 30 minutes. You can utilize any pie filling (in spite of the fact that I think blueberry is the best).

Oil, for spraying
2 cups universally handy flour
¼ teaspoon baking soda
¼ teaspoon salt
½ cup vegetable oil
⅓ cup buttermilk
1 (21-ounce) can blueberry pie filling
1 huge egg, beaten
1 cup confectioners' sugar
2 tablespoons milk

1. Line the air fryer crate with material and shower softly with oil.
2. In an enormous bowl, combine as one the flour, baking pop, and salt. Add the vegetable oil and buttermilk and combine as one until the combination shapes a ball.
3. Roll out the mixture on a work surface until it is about ¼ inch thick. Utilizing a 4-inch bread roll shaper or the edge of a glass, cut 12 circles. You might have to reroll the pieces of mixture to get 12 circles.
4. Spoon a bit of pie filling in the focal point of every batter circle.
5. Fill a little bowl with water. Utilizing your fingers, wet the edges of the mixture with water. Crease the mixture down the middle and press the

edges with a fork to seal it closed.
6. Brush the pies with the egg. Utilizing a fork, punch little holes in the highest point of each pie.
7. Place the pies in the pre-arranged bushel, taking consideration not to cover, and splash delicately with oil. You might have to cook in groups, contingent upon the size of your air fryer.
8. Cook at 350°F for 10 minutes, or until brilliant brown. Let cool completely.
9. In a little bowl, whisk together the confectioners' sugar and milk and set aside.
10. Have a piece of material paper or an enormous plate close by. Dunk the pies in the coating blend, going to cover the two sides. Utilize a fork to lift them out of the bowl and to help shake off any overabundance. Place them on the material and let the frosting dry before serving.

Faster Frying: You can likewise utilize a defrosted sheet of frozen puffed cake as opposed to making the batter from scratch.

Per serving (1 pie): Calories: 290; Total fat: 10g; Saturated fat: 1g; Cholesterol: 16mg; Sodium: 96mg; Carbohydrates: 47g; Fiber: 2g; Protein: 3g

CAN YOU AIR FRY IT?

PINEAPPLE

Line the air fryer basket with parchment and spray lightly with oil. Cut a pineapple into spears and place in the prepared basket. Brush with melted butter and cook at 400°F for 5 to 6 minutes. Brush with more butter and cook for another 5 to 6 minutes, or until the pineapple is hot and the natural sugars are bubbling. These make a simple but special dessert or snack.

BERRY CHEESECAKE

FAMILY FAVORITE
GLUTEN-FREE
VEGETARIAN

Serves 4/Prep Time: 5 minutes, in addition to 2 hours to chill/Fry Time: 10 minutes

Who realized you could make a cheesecake without any preparation in around 15 minutes? A few cheesecake plans take the better piece of a day to get ready, however this one is staggeringly basic, particularly assuming that you utilize a blender to blend the ingredients.
This adaptation has no outside layer, yet you won't miss it-or the additional calories.

Oil, for spraying
8 ounces cream cheddar
6 tablespoons sugar
1 tablespoon harsh cream
1 huge egg
½ teaspoon vanilla extract
¼ teaspoon lemon juice
½ cup new blended berries

1. Preheat the air fryer to 350°F. Line the air fryer bin with material and splash gently with oil.
2. In a blender, join the cream cheddar, sugar, harsh cream, egg, vanilla, and lemon squeeze and mix until smooth. Empty the combination into a 4-inch springform pan.
3. Place the dish in the arranged basket.
4. Cook for 8 to 10 minutes, or until just the extremely focus shakes marginally when the skillet is moved.
5. Refrigerate the cheesecake in the search for gold least 2 hours.
6. Release the sides from the springform container, top the cheesecake with the blended berries, and serve.

Change It Up: Instead of organic product, have a go at garnish the cheesecake with chocolate ganache, caramel sauce, or a sprinkle of squashed treats or toffee.

Per serving: Calories: 300; Total fat: 21g; Saturated fat: 11g; Cholesterol: 105mg; Sodium: 224mg; Carbohydrates: 24g; Fiber: 0g; Protein: 5g

MERINGUE COOKIES

FAMILY FAVORITE
GLUTEN-FREE
VEGETARIAN

Makes 20 treats/Prep Time: 15 minutes/Fry Time: 1 hour 30 minutes

Light, vaporous, and emphatically flavorful meringue treats are a characteristic for the air fryer.

Oil, for splashing
4 enormous egg
whites 1 cup
sugar
Pinch cream of tartar

1. Preheat the air fryer to 140°F. Line the air fryer crate with material and shower gently with oil.
2. In a little heatproof bowl, whisk together the egg whites and sugar. Fill a little pot most of the way with water, place it over medium hotness, and bring to a light stew. Place the bowl with the egg whites on the pan, ensuring the lower part of the bowl doesn't contact the water. Whisk the combination until the sugar is dissolved.
3. Transfer the blend to a huge bowl and add the cream of tartar. Utilizing an electric blender, beat the combination on high until it is polished and solid pinnacles structure. Move the combination to a channeling pack or a zip-top plastic sack with a corner cut off.
4. Pipe adjusts into the pre-arranged container. You might have to work in bunches, contingent upon the size of your air fryer.
5. Cook for 1 hour 30 minutes.
6. Turn behind closed doors fryer and let the meringues cool totally inside. The leftover hotness will keep on drying them out.

Fry Fact: The treats are done when they are fresh outwardly and lift from the material without staying. They should sound empty when tapped on the base. Dampness ruins meringues, so make certain to store them in a hermetically sealed container.

Per serving (2 treats): Calories: 84; Total fat: 0g; Saturated fat: 0g; Cholesterol: 0mg; Sodium: 22mg; Carbohydrates: 20g; Fiber: 0g; Protein: 1g

SHORTBREAD COOKIE STICKS

FAMILY FAVORITE
VEGETARIAN

Serves 4/Prep Time: 10 minutes/Fry Time: 10 minutes

This exemplary Scottish bread roll treat is rich sweet and has just three fixings. The air fryer diminishes the typical baking time by 25 minutes, so you can appreciate them nearly when the hankering strikes. Present with evening tea or give them as gifts during the holidays.

Oil, for spraying
2 cups self-rising flour
¾ cup (1½ sticks) unsalted margarine, cubed
⅔ cup confectioners' sugar

1. Line the air fryer bushel with material and shower gently with oil.
2. In an enormous bowl, combine as one the flour, spread, and confectioners' sugar with your hands until it takes after thick bread morsels. Keep on manipulating until the blend shapes a mixture ball.
3. On a work surface, carry out the batter until it is ¼ to ½ inch thick.
4. Using a sharp blade or a pizza wheel, slice the mixture into 3-to 4-inch-long sticks.
5. Place the sticks in the pre-arranged crate. You might have to work in clumps, contingent upon the size of your air fryer.
6. Cook at 360°F for 10 minutes. On the off chance that you need the shortbread to be more brilliant brown, cook for an additional 2 minutes. Let cool totally on the material before serving.

Fry Fact: Be mindful so as not to exhaust the mixture, which will cause a lot of gluten to frame and bring about a chewier treat. You can make self-rising flour by consolidating 1 cup universally handy flour with 2 teaspoons baking powder.

Per serving: Calories: 592; Total fat: 35g; Saturated fat: 22g; Cholesterol: 92mg; Sodium: 942mg; Carbohydrates: 63g; Fiber: 2g; Protein: 7g

CHOCOLATE-STUFFED WONTONS

FAMILY FAVORITE
VEGETARIAN

Makes 24 wontons/Prep Time: 10 minutes/Fry Time: 10 minutes

Although wontons are normally loaded down with exquisite food varieties, the firm, crunchy singed coverings are similarly as heavenly when matched with sweet ingredients.
These overwhelming treats are loaded up with velvety chocolate and cleaned with confectioners' sugar.

Oil, for spraying
8 ounces cream cheese
½ cup granulated sugar
¼ cup unsweetened cocoa powder
1 teaspoon almond extract
24 wonton wrappers
¼ cup confectioners' sugar

1. Line the air fryer crate with material and shower softly with oil.
2. In a huge bowl, combine as one the cream cheddar, granulated sugar, cocoa powder, and almond extricate until creamy.
3. Lay the wonton coverings on a work surface and spot 1 tablespoon of the chocolate filling in the focal point of each one.
4. Fill a little bowl with water. Plunge your finger in the water and soak the external edges of every covering. Overlay the wonton down the middle, corner to corner, and squeeze the edges together to seal.
5. Place the wontons in the pre-arranged bin and shower with oil. You might have to work in clusters, contingent upon the size of your air fryer.
6. Cook at 350°F for 5 minutes, shake, splash with oil, and cook for an additional 5 minutes, until crispy.
7. Dust with the confectioners' sugar before serving.

Change It Up: Replace the chocolate loading up with chocolate-hazelnut spread or peanut butter for an alternate flavor twist.

Per serving (2 wontons): Calories: 159; Total fat: 7g; Saturated fat: 4g; Cholesterol: 22mg; Sodium: 161mg; Carbohydrates: 21g; Fiber: 1g; Protein: 3g

CHOCOLATE LAVA CAKES

FAMILY FAVORITE
VEGETARIAN

Makes 4 cakes/Prep Time: 7 minutes/Fry Time: 12 minutes

Lava cakes have a hot, gooey fudgy focus that slimes out when cut open. They can be served plain or with a cleaning of confectioners' sugar, or you can make them fancier for visitors with an embellishment of new berries, whipped cream, chocolate sauce, and a branch of mint.

Oil, for greasing
⅔ cup semisweet chocolate chips
8 tablespoons (1 stick) unsalted margarine,
cubed 1 cup confectioners' sugar
2 huge eggs in addition to 2 huge egg yolks, at room
temperature 1 teaspoon vanilla extract
6 tablespoons universally handy flour
4 scoops vanilla frozen yogurt, for serving
Chocolate syrup, for serving

1. Preheat the air fryer to 375°F. Oil 4 ramekins and set aside.
2. In a microwave-safe bowl, consolidate the chocolate chips and spread and microwave on high for 30 to 45 seconds, or until the chocolate is melted.
3. Add the confectioners' sugar, eggs, egg yolks, and vanilla and rush to join. Crease in the flour.
4. Divide the hitter equitably among the ramekins and spot them out of sight fryer.
5. Cook for 10 to 12 minutes, or until the inside temperature arrives at 160°F.
6. Let represent 5 minutes. Reverse the ramekins onto individual plates. Top with frozen yogurt and a sprinkle of chocolate syrup before serving.

Fry Fact: Fryer temps can differ extraordinarily, particularly with regards to baking, so make a point to actually look at the temperature at the edge of the cakes. The middle won't give you an exact temperature.

Per serving (1 cake): Calories: 821; Total fat: 46g; Saturated fat: 27g; Cholesterol: 277mg; Sodium: 307mg; Carbohydrates: 90g; Fiber: 4g; Protein: 11g

OVERLOAD DESSERT PIZZA

FAMILY FAVORITE
VEGETARIAN

Serves 4/Prep Time: 8 minutes/Fry Time: 13 minutes

A monster treat stacked with candy is a dependable method for winning enormous grins. This formula is an ideal method for spending extra sweets, and it makes a pleasant action during sleepovers. Partake in this treat with a glass of cold milk.

Oil, for greasing
4 tablespoons unsalted margarine, at room temperature
¼ cup granulated sugar
¼ cup stuffed light brown sugar
½ large egg (see <u>Fry Fact</u>)
½ teaspoon vanilla extract
¾ cup generally useful flour
¼ teaspoon baking soda
⅛ teaspoon salt
½ cup semisweet chocolate chips
1 cup cleaved pieces of candy and candies

1. Preheat the air fryer to 350°F. Oil a 6-or 7-inch round metal cake container, contingent upon the size of your air fryer.
2. In an enormous bowl, beat the spread, granulated sugar, and earthy colored sugar with an electric blender until rich. Add the egg and vanilla and beat until combined.
3. Add the flour, baking pop, and salt and beat until smooth. Overlay in the chocolate chips.
4. Press the batter into the arranged pan.
5. Cook for 9 to 11 minutes, or until daintily seared around the edges. Top with the cleaved sweets and cook for one more 1 to 2 minutes, or until the candy is marginally dissolved. Cut into cuts and serve immediately.

Fry Fact: To quantify a large portion of an egg, break 1 egg into a little bowl and whisk well with a fork. Measure out 1½ tablespoons to use in the batter, disposing of the rest of. You can likewise utilize 2 tablespoons of
sanitized egg product.

Per serving: Calories: 486; Total fat: 24g; Saturated fat: 13g; Cholesterol: 53mg; Sodium: 293mg; Carbohydrates: 64g; Fiber: 3g; Protein: 6g

CHOCOLATE MUG CAKES

SUPER-FAST
VEGETARIAN

Makes 1 cake/Prep Time: 2 minutes/Fry Time: 13 minutes

Sometimes you're needing a tiny bit of piece of cake, yet you would rather not go the entire day in the kitchen or have a great deal of extras. This is the place where mug cakes come in. These individual size pastries are prepared in minutes.

Oil, for spraying
6 tablespoons chocolate cake mix
2 tablespoons unsweetened fruit purée
1 tablespoon water

1. Line the air fryer bushel with material and splash softly with oil.
2. In a 8-ounce mug, whisk together the cake blend, fruit purée, and water until smooth.
3. Place the mug in the arranged basket.
4. Cook at 350°F for 12 to 13 minutes, or until the cake is puffed up and the top springs back when squeezed with your finger.
5. Let cool for a couple of moments before serving.

Change It Up: This formula will make either 1 (8-ounce) mug or 2 (4-ounce) ramekins and can be made with any flavor cake blend. You can twofold this formula, yet blend the fixings in isolated mugs to guarantee each mug has a similar sum and they cook consistently.

Per serving (1 cake): Calories: 235; Total fat: 5g; Saturated fat: 1g; Cholesterol: 0mg; Sodium: 376mg; Carbohydrates: 49g; Fiber: 2g; Protein: 3g

CAN YOU AIR FRY IT?

BROWNIE MIX

If your fryer is big enough to fit an 8-inch square pan, prepare the mix according to the package directions and pour into the greased pan. Cook at 325°F for 18 to 22 minutes, or until a toothpick inserted into the center comes out clean.

AIR FRYER COOKING CHARTS:
FROZEN AND FRESH FOODS

The main explanation I'm fixated on my air fryer is that it is so adaptable. You can make nearly anything you would typically cook in an ordinary broiler. Furthermore some of the time that implies frozen food. The accompanying diagram records the cook times for a few frozen top picks for a speedy weeknight feast. It additionally has cook times for an assortment of new food varieties, which you can use as a helpful cheat sheet for making your own air-singed manifestations. Note: These occasions have been tried utilizing an additional an enormous bin style fryer.

FROZEN FOODS

FROZEN FOOD	QUANTITY	TIME	TEMPERATURE	NOTES
Breaded shrimp	Up to ½ pound	8 to 10 minutes	400°F	Spray with oil and flip halfway through cooking
Burgers	1 or 2 patties	14 to 15 minutes	400°F	Do not stack; flip halfway through cooking
Burritos	1 or 2 burritos	8 to 10 minutes	400°F	Spray with oil and flip halfway through cooking
Chicken nuggets	6 to 12 pieces	10 to 15 minutes	400°F	Spray with oil and shake halfway through cooking
Egg rolls	3 or 4 egg rolls	3 to 6 minutes	390°F	Brush or spray with oil before cooking
Fish fillet	1 or 2 pieces	14 to 15 minutes	400°F	Spray with oil and flip halfway through cooking
Fish sticks	6 to 12 pieces	6 to 10 minutes	400°F	Spray with oil and shake halfway through cooking
Hash browns	1 or 2 pieces	15 to 18 minutes	370°F	Spray with oil and shake halfway through cooking
Meatballs	5 to 10 meatballs	8 to 10 minutes	380°F	Flip halfway through cooking

Mozzarella sticks	4 to 8 sticks	8 to 10 minutes	360°F	Spray with oil and flip halfway through cooking
Onion rings	½ pound	8 to 10 minutes	400°F	Spray with oil and flip halfway through cooking
Pizza	½ pizza	5 minutes to 10	390°F	Place pizza on parchment paper; make sure it fits in the basket
Pizza bagels	2 or 3 pizza bagels	8 to 10 minutes	375°F	Spray with oil; do not stack
Pizza rolls (bites)	5 to 10 pizza rolls	5 to 7 minutes	375°F	Spray with oil and shake halfway through cooking
Pot stickers	5 to 10 pot stickers	8 to 10 minutes	400°F	Spray with oil and flip halfway through cooking
Samosas	3 or 4 samosas	5 to 10 minutes	400°F	Spray with oil and shake halfway through cooking
Tater tots	10 to 20 tots	10 to 12 minutes	400°F	Spray with oil and shake halfway through cooking
Thick fries	10 to 20 fries	18 to 20 minutes	400°F	Spray with oil and shake halfway through cooking
Thin fries	10 to 20 fries	14 minutes	400°F	Spray with oil and shake halfway through cooking

FRESH VEGETABLES

FRESH VEGETABLE	QUANTITY	TIME	TEMPERATURE	NOTES
Asparagus	½ pound	5 to 8 minutes	400°F	Trim ends before cooking; spray with oil and sprinkle with seasonings
Broccoli	1 to 2 cups	5 to 8 minutes	400°F	Spray with oil and sprinkle with seasonings
Brussels sprouts	1 cup	13 minutes to 15	380°F	Cut in half before cooking; spray with oil and sprinkle with seasonings
Carrots	½ to 1 cup	7 to 10 minutes	380°F	Cut first; spray with oil and sprinkle with seasonings
Cauliflower florets	1 to 2 cups	9 to 10 minutes	360°F	Spray with oil and sprinkle with seasonings
Corn on the cob	2 ears	6 minutes	390°F	Spray with oil and sprinkle with seasonings

Vegetable	Quantity	Time	Temperature	Notes
Eggplant	½ to 2 pounds	13 to 15 minutes	400°F	Spray with oil and flip halfway through cooking
Green beans	½ to 1 pound	5 minutes	400°F	Spray with oil and shake halfway through cooking
Kale	½ bunch	10 minutes to 12	275°F	Trim leaves from the ribs; spray with oil and sprinkle with seasonings
Mushrooms	½ to 1 cup	5 to 8 minutes	400°F	Trim stems first; sprinkle with seasonings
Onions	½ pound to 1	5 to 8 minutes	370°F	Cut first
Peppers (bell)	½ to 1 cup	minutes 6 to 8	370°F	Cut first
Potatoes (baked)	1 to 2 pounds	40 minutes	400°F	Poke holes first; spray with oil and sprinkle with seasonings
Potatoes (cubed)	1 to 2 cups	15 minutes	400°F	Spray with oil and shake halfway through cooking
Potatoes (fries)	1 to 2 cups	15 minutes	380°F	Spray with oil and shake halfway through cooking
Potatoes (wedges)	1 to 3 cups	18 to 20 minutes	380°F	Spray with oil and shake halfway through cooking
Squash	½ pound	12 to 13 minutes	400°F	Spray with oil and sprinkle with seasonings
Sweet potatoes (baked)	1 large or 2 small sweet potatoes	35 to 40 minutes	390°F	Poke holes first; spray with oil and sprinkle with seasonings
Sweet potatoes (cubed)	1 to 3 cups	14 to 20 minutes	380°F	Spray with oil and shake halfway through cooking
Sweet potatoes (fries)	1 to 2 cups	25 minutes	380°F	Spray with oil and shake halfway through cooking
Tomatoes (breaded)	1 or 2 tomatoes	10 minutes	350°F	Cut first; season or bread and spray with oil
Zucchini	½ to 1 pound	10 to 12 minutes	370°F	Cut first; spray with oil and sprinkle with seasonings

FRESH CHICKEN

CHICKEN	QUANTITY	TIME	TEMPERATURE	NOTES

Chicken breasts (boneless, skinless)	1 or 2 (6-ounce) breasts	12 to 15 minutes	380°F	Spray with oil; sprinkle with seasonings and flip halfway through cooking
Chicken drumettes	1 to 4 drumettes	20 minutes	400°F	Spray with oil; sprinkle with seasonings and shake halfway through cooking
Chicken drumsticks	1 to 4 drumsticks	16 to 20 minutes	390°F	Spray with oil; sprinkle with seasonings and shake halfway through cooking
Chicken thighs (bone-in)	1 or 2 (6-ounce) thighs	22 minutes	380°F	Spray with oil; sprinkle with seasonings and shake halfway through cooking
Chicken thighs (boneless)	1 or 2 (6-ounce) thighs	18 to 20 minutes	380°F	Spray with oil; sprinkle with seasonings and flip halfway through cooking
Chicken tenders	1 to 4 tenders	8 to 10 minutes	375°F	Spray with oil; sprinkle with seasonings and shake halfway through cooking
Chicken wings	1 to 4 wings	15 to 20 minutes	400°F	Spray with oil; sprinkle with seasonings and shake halfway through cooking
Whole chicken	4 pounds	1 hour 15 minutes	360°F	Spray with oil; sprinkle with seasonings

FRESH BEEF

BEEF	**QUANTITY**	**TIME**	**TEMPERATURE**	**NOTES**
Burgers	1 or 2 patties	8 to 10 minutes	400°F	Do not stack; flip halfway through cooking
Filet mignon	1 or 2 (6-ounce) steaks	8 to 10 minutes	360°F	Time will vary depending on the desired doneness; use a meat thermometer and cook to 125°F for rare, 135°F for medium-rare, 145°F for medium, 155°F for medium-well, and 160°F for well-done
Flank steak	¼ to ½ pound	8 to 10 minutes	360°F	Time will vary depending on the desired doneness; use a meat thermometer and cook to 125°F for rare, 135°F for medium-rare, 145°F for medium, 155°F for medium-well, and 160°F for well-done

Meatballs	5 to 10 meatballs	7 to 10 minutes	380°F	Sprinkle with seasonings and flip halfway through cooking
Ribeye	1 or 2 (6-ounce) steaks	10 to 15 minutes	380°F	Time will vary depending on the desired doneness; use a meat thermometer and cook to 125°F for rare, 135°F for medium-rare, 145°F for medium, 155°F for medium-well, and 160°F for well-done
Sirloin steak	1 or 2 (6-ounce) steaks	12 to 14 minutes	400°F	Time will vary depending on the desired doneness; use a meat thermometer and cook to 125°F for rare, 135°F for medium-rare, 145°F for medium, 155°F for medium-well, and 160°F for well-done

FRESH PORK AND LAMB

PORK AND LAMB	QUANTITY	TIME	TEMPERATURE	NOTES
Bacon	2 to 4 slices	7 to 10 minutes	400°F	Flip halfway through cooking
Lamb chops	¼ to ½ pound	10 to 12 minutes	400°F	Do not stack; sprinkle with seasonings; flip halfway through cooking
Pork chops (bone-in or boneless)	¼ to ½ pound	12 to 15 minutes	380°F	Spray with oil; sprinkle with seasonings and flip halfway through cooking
Pork loin	¼ to ½ pound	50 to 60 minutes	360°F	Spray with oil; sprinkle with seasonings and flip halfway through cooking
Pork tenderloin	¼ to ½ pound	12 to 15 minutes	390°F	Spray with oil; sprinkle with seasonings and cook whole
Rack of lamb	¼ to ½ pound	22 to 25 minutes	380°F	Do not stack; flip halfway through cooking
Sausage (links)	¼ to ½ pound	13 to 15 minutes	380°F	Pierce holes in sausages first
Sausage (patties)	1 to 4 patties	13 to 15 minutes	380°F	Flip halfway through cooking

FRESH FISH AND SHELLFISH

FISH AND SHELLFISH	QUANTITY	TIME	TEMPERATURE	NOTES

Crab cakes	1 or 2 cakes	8 minutes to 10	375°F	Toss with cornstarch; spray with oil; sprinkle with seasonings
Fish fillets	¼ to ½ pound	10 to 12 minutes	320°F	Spray with oil; sprinkle with seasonings
Scallops	¼ to ½ pound	5 to 7 minutes	320°F	Spray with oil; sprinkle with seasonings
Shrimp	¼ to ½ pound	7 to 8 minutes	400°F	Peel and devein; spray with oil; sprinkle with seasonings

FRESH FRUIT

FRESH FRUIT	QUANTITY	TIME	TEMPERATURE	NOTES
Apples	1 to 3 cups	4 to 7 minutes	350°F	Cut first
Bananas	1 to 3 cups	4 to 7 minutes	350°F	Cut first
Peaches	1 to 3 cups	5 to 6 minutes	350°F	Cut first

MEASUREMENT CONVERSIONS

VOLUME EQUIVALENTS	US Standard	US Standard (ounces)	Metric (approximate)
LIQUID	2 tablespoons	1 fl. oz.	30 mL
	¼ cup	2 fl. oz.	60 mL
	½ cup	4 fl. oz.	120 mL
	1 cup	8 fl. oz.	240 mL
	1½ cups	12 fl. oz.	355 mL
	2 cups or 1 pint	16 fl. oz.	475 mL
	4 cups or 1 quart	32 fl. oz.	1 L
	1 gallon	128 fl. oz.	4 L
DRY	⅛ teaspoon	—	0.5 mL
	¼ teaspoon	—	1 mL
	½ teaspoon	—	2 mL
	¾ teaspoon	—	4 mL
	1 teaspoon	—	5 mL
	1 tablespoon	—	15 mL
	¼ cup	—	59 mL
	⅓ cup	—	79 mL
	½ cup	—	118 mL
	⅔ cup	—	156 mL
	¾ cup	—	177 mL
	1 cup	—	235 mL
	2 cups or 1 pint	—	475 mL
	3 cups	—	700 mL
	4 cups or 1 quart	—	1 L
	½ gallon	—	2 L
	1 gallon	—	4 L

OVEN TEMPERATURES

Fahrenheit	Celsius (approximate)
250°F	120°C
300°F	150°C
325°F	165°C
350°F	180°C
375°F	190°C
400°F	200°C
425°F	220°C
450°F	230°C

WEIGHT EQUIVALENTS

US Standard	Metric (approximate)
½ ounce	15 g
1 ounce	30 g
2 ounces	60 g
4 ounces	115 g
8 ounces	225 g
12 ounces	340 g
16 ounces or 1 pound	455 g

Printed in Great Britain
by Amazon